To Run

Redefining Purpose in Changing Seasons of Life

DAN BILLISH

To Run

Peace Project Publishing

Library of Congress Cataloging-in-Publication Data is available upon request.

ISBN: 9781079998900

Cover design: Eric S. Anderson

Second Edition
10 9 8 7 6 5 4 3 2 1

PRINTED IN THE UNITED STATES OF AMERICA

To Run

Dedication

This book would have no legs minus the life altering coaches I have been blessed to work with: Jack Bolton, Don Molenda, Bill Gleeson, Sam Bell, Marshall Goss and Dr. Robert Chapman. Each of them contributed a verse to my story and I am eternally grateful for the father-figures who kept tabs on me even in the most difficult times.

To my teammates, your impact was just as great. I thank you for your friendship and challenge. Without you, my chaotic mind may have led me down a different path. The community you created remains something embedded in my being and the love I have for you cannot be quantified.

To Run

To Run

CONTENTS

To Run

Acknowledgements

Foremost, thank you to God for writing this story. You are the greatest author of all time.

To my wife Renee for tolerating my writing and editing and writing and editing. You were the first set of eyes on this manuscript and I appreciate your contribution and feedback.

To my sons, Cayden and Lincoln, you can't read yet, but one day, this book will tell you a little more about your father's journey.

To my parents and family for always reminding me I am fortunate and loved.

To my past and current students/athletes, thank you for delivering purpose in my journey home.

To my friends from St. John Fisher, Brother Rice, Indiana University, and beyond, I appreciate you.

To everyone that has crossed my path and left footprints on my heart and soul, thank you for bringing me to the realization of who I am.

To Run

Introduction

Why do I run?

When I graduated from high school, the experiences and opportunities presented were life giving and left me with a remarkable base to take into the next stage of life. Just four years' prior, naming a school as a second home seemed an impossibility as I was trending more into oblivion than blending with any social environment. These fortunate events shaped me in many avenues of my life. From my entrance as disorderly to a well-rounded exit, Brother Rice High School, on the south side of Chicago, was as stable a base I could have asked for. School concluded before my track & field season did leaving my memories surrounding the state championships. I managed a personal record (PR) and school record in my last 800-meter contest aligning with the storybook ending I would have preferred. It took years for me to realize my talent and I felt ready for the next level of commitment at the collegiate level, although I was unaware of what that would entail. This transition did not come without doubts. Even though my trajectory pointed upwards, the sell of running was not final.

To Run

I often wondered what my life would have been like without running. A quick gaze at my surroundings and it is clear that running defines me in some form. My basement tells a life story through items that symbolize my met goals in running and those I shared them with. A pretty picture to me now, but there were many phases of my life when I would drift to a place where running was not my priority. It relaxed me as I would daydream about the new-found freedom minus the rigorous training schedule. Many days in my competitive years, the phone ringing with day long or weekend plans would create a circulation of doubt about my commitment to such a futile thing. These were the times it hampered me with plans of a workout and the needed rest to complete the run successfully. My mind quickly threw out the barricades: I need rest, I must hydrate, any physical activity will only make my run more difficult. Was this sacrifice worth it? Just thinking about the parameters of such a life would cause my stress level to elevate. Fun times awaited, but my stubborn training schedule spoke of guilt.

Another opportunity turned down to enjoy the company of my friends because I had to do what was expected of me. I concluded that running was my life. It helped me become more patient and more productive in the classroom, but I often thought some other activity would have provided me with much the same. The constant of a routine schedule plagued me, but what did I miss? I ran close to 350 days of the year and for what? An All-State selection, Big Ten title or NCAA bid? It seems absurd, but the most vivid memories I have are of these events, not graduation or a family vacation, but a single race or season. Running made me feel invincible even if just for a moment.

It's interesting how life works. In my early days, all the toil and pain were to fulfill some other person's presumed expectations of me. Is that what people are driven by or was it just me? I benefitted for sure evolving both as a runner and as a person. I am thankful for my talents and I enjoy always having a story to tell. Some days I wished that my talents were less, that I could have lived without pressure and expectation. A day when I could sit around and not feel guilty about a missed or poor workout. A day when I could go with my friends for an extended period without planning when and where I would run. A day when athleticism did not take center stage over my ability to contribute to the good of humankind.

After countless years of missed opportunities, the only reflection I have of accomplishments are dusty medals, dismembered trophies, stacked plaques that litter the storage space in my home, and my memories. Oh, the memories! Most of my memories have a basis in running, but that is not the whole picture. Because my life centered on running, all social and familial paths circulated around it. Many

3

transformative relationships were initiated through this environment that forgetting the "when and where" of these events is nearly impossible. I remember the state championships perfectly, the Big Ten Championships, NCAA's, yet the races are not the story; they are the setting. All my running adventures were the genesis of life, a place God put me to grow. Who am I? Most would say a runner despite my frame no longer resembling the quintessential definition of. I am forever associated with running and I am blessed. Many people would say I missed out, on what I am not sure, but sometimes the lifestyle became hectic and my mind would wander to greater simplicity. Have I lived a full life, or have I missed out on something integral to my development as a person? It has happened before, consumed entirely by something only to find that it was not a fit. Maybe this was all part of the majestic plan from the onset.

Many of these questions circulated in my mind during different seasons of my life. I would often question the events and the experiences that reflected or molded me as a person. The number of times I questioned direction are many. Whether it was my transition of sport, the lagging college experience, a short-lived post collegiate career, in the ranks of coaching or in my professional life, I always reevaluated my circumstances. The most difficult part of my journey was in deciding to do things that would make me happy and not to please someone else. I'm sure we are all guilty of it, mimicking another's path or people copying, because, at the most basic level, we wanted to fit... somewhere and with someone. Now, many years past my competitive days, I know I took the right path and the sacrifices... well, they feel little like sacrifices. This is the lens from which I experienced life.

To Run

PART ONE

Spring

To Run

Weathered

As I sat outside on my deck awaiting the oncoming storm, something almost as potent as lightning struck me. I observed the behaviors of the trees sitting before me, swaying in the wind with the front rolling in. My mind began to settle into a haze as the first drops of rain struck the grass that lied at my feet, but I was so entranced by the tree I barely noticed. My attention climbed this structure as I witnessed the leaves reaching to the sky with the hopeful wish of nourishment. Some achieved their desire while others detached spiraling to the ground. How does a tree grow from a small stick in the mud to an amazing sight reaching to the heavens? It has endured many storms, but it continues to grow and blossom every spring. I realized runners share a lot in common with trees. We train and test our bodies, sometimes even losing parts of ourselves, but once again, there is a rebirth of sorts, a springtime. We trudge through all-weather continuing to advance and mature becoming massive in stature. We may crack, sometimes we burn and sometimes we go bare, yet we remain standing. There may be times when things just do not seem to get any better and we are barren of our prior fortress of leaves. Our heads remain raised longing for the day when life will fill us again. Our times of esteem thrive and then quickly die, but it does not hamper us as we continue to return to what we love. With each storm that rattles us, our roots continue to expand. We are unshakable because of being weathered.

In the Beginning

My life resembles that of a roller coaster. There are many peaks and valleys, but during my younger years, there seemed to be a constant of less memorable times. When people meet me, they see a person who has a handful of good in his life. Even though there are times today I feel things could not be better, my past contested if things could get any worse. I was raised on the south side of Chicago in the Beverly neighborhood. It was an Irish Catholic community on the furthest edge of the city. My memories take me back to 104th and Campbell Avenue where my journey began. As a child I was a nuisance to my teachers and family, although I am sure my family will not admit to the fact, but I know in my heart I hurt many people. I had a very short temper and insisted that things always went the way I had planned. Although I have achieved a great deal of balance, there was a time when equilibrium was a distant reality.

In elementary school, I was of the mind that the world should curve to appease me, or an episode was soon to follow. I recall an incident from second grade where I was known as the class clown. A sense of purpose came with this title because it was the one thing that would get me attention. The teacher had just left the room to have a discussion with another teacher in the hallway when the tents went up and the circus began. I stood on the desk and waited for the class's astonishment and cheers. Every time I felt I had a minute when the teacher was not looking, I returned to the desktop. With the encouragement from the class, my stand on the desk routine continued. Unfortunately for me, blinded by the attention, I stood up again for an endless period. The class eruption was so great that the teacher quickly returned as I was attempting to dismount the desk. She ordered me to go directly to the principal's office, which was much like a second home for me, but I resisted. I grabbed the vintage, 300 pound, cement desk as the teacher attempted to pry my hands from its grasp. She was unsuccessful and left the hopeless case alone for the time being and instead continued the class.

This incident triggered a series of evaluations that began to hamper me beyond the constraints of the classroom. My teachers and parents decided that I would have a behavior evaluation comprised of a check, check minus, and check plus. At the end of each day, I would go to each teacher's room and have them fill out the form. If my report was positive, my parents would allow me to go out after school, but if not, they grounded me. Despite some progress being made because of my new "anti-grounding motivation" at school, things at home worsened.

I come from a loving family where my parents did everything in their power to provide my sisters and I with the best childhood they could. I did not want that; I wanted more. I wanted all the attention, all the time. Later, we learned that my left-prefrontal cortical activity was lagging, so it skewed my motivational direction. A diagnosis unfortunately was not the solution as continued development of the left side of my brain would correct itself by the simple remedy of time. They told my parents I had anger issues; the solution was to wait it out. There was no designated end to my behavior, and it remains the most selfish period of my life. This constant battle became the regular cycle of events in our household to offset a meltdown.

As a child, I was unaware that getting my way would have such a detrimental cost. When my father was around, I often kept to myself, but my father worked almost endless hours to raise his business. With his absence, my feverish temperament exploded. I was physically violent with myself. For some unknown reason, my rationale was that I was the only one being hurt. If I could have only processed the tears I watched run down my mother's face, I wouldn't hold on to so much regret. Today my mother is still my top supporter, and her love for me has never ceased. She has instilled in me the gifts of patience and unadulterated love for all no matter how much pain they put you through. Much of this message came because of being raised Catholic. Our family was very much a part of the fabric of the church and community.

My parents led a teen youth group that convened at our house weekly and spent much time in charitable giving in person and monetarily. I had models for certain despite my lack of obedience, yet the imprint of their faith and commitment to others turned my heart in that direction over the years. As a parent, I have witnessed heart melting love from my children and complete dysfunction. Regardless of the headaches initiated by our boys, I only have one option in proper rearing, love. It would not surprise me in the least if my parents found some satisfaction in me getting thrown through the ringer from time to time by our dynamic duo. The amazing part about it is that their love only grew; the more I progressed, the more rewarded they became. In my profession as a high school educator, I can honestly say I want my students to grow, to learn, and to feel loved. The learned behavior of short-term memory has allowed me to view each day as its own chapter. Even though the love could have been withheld, and rightfully so, it was not. The continual reinforcement of such standards led me to echo those ideals as I grew in maturity.

The world changes with children and the lessons affirmed in my childhood resonate in the understanding that there is never a reason to give up on someone. I am the poster child. Every person possesses an ability to contribute to life in a meaningful way, but we must instill self-worth. That does not mean that the entire world will see your unique talents but expose them anyway. Some of the most rewarding responses to issued love were not even on my radar. I did not understand the length of my impact. That is the beauty, so why limit yourself? My parents exemplified this and have continued to support me to this day. I only wish I am returning the favor in some form. My father has always been there to tell me things straight with no additives and my mother is the Energizer Bunny of humans, her love keeps going and going... A tainted emotion blinded my childhood to realize everything they gave me. The only tempering of my outlandish behavior was in athletic form, and the gross amount of lessons that came with it had a life altering effect.

To Run

Running Roots

In 1987, I was nine years old, and the seed was planted that would continue to grow over the years. I come from a family with a long history in running. When I was younger, I went to my cousin Mike's high school cross country meet. Although I remember nothing about the race per se, it presented the opportunity to run. As my father was in conversation with my Uncle Dick, I overheard them mention "the girls", my twin older sisters, potential involvement in formal running. Little did I know this singular experience would transform my life. My uncle quickly referenced them to Jack Bolton. Jack governed the Marquette Park Track Club and was a legendary miler from Ireland. As I overheard the conversation, I decided that I wanted to run too, well at least in as much to continue to mirror my sisters. Ever since I was young, I always wanted to do whatever my sisters were doing; this situation was much the same. My cousin ran for the club and this also began my shadowing of him. It was an introduction to a new expectation. Coach Jack was always an old man to me, 70 years young, with an Irish brogue that instilled fear and commanded respect. He became the first voice of the sport in my life. This exposure to an "old school" coaching mentality was a key ingredient in my development. I may have been ignorant to discipline in other arenas, but not in athletics. Here, I was a sponge, I did what I was told without question.

In the following weeks, the Billish trio was off to 63rd and Kedzie, surmounting the south Kedzie overpass bridge; our noses met the scents of the Nabisco factory and our eyes the landscape of Marquette Park. Upon arrival, I had not thought about the miles of pain in front of us since my purpose for being there was not born out of a passion to run. It became clear as I picked up the motivational chatter of my newfound coach, that the direct focus was winning a national championship. The governance of the time was The Athletics Congress (TAC), which later was coined the USATF. All our energies aligned to this singular end, the TAC Championships. No small feat that this was now the task in front of a kid at his first day of practice. The most appropriate definition for me would have been "lost". I really didn't know why I was there, what it would take to race, maybe win a national title, while encircling this gargantuan park without literally getting lost.

The memory of Marquette Park will not fade. There was a trail that encompassed the enormous park and we would loop around until complete darkness. I could not map out where I ran, but I can recall those days vividly. We met at a cinder track where we would begin our runs. I was unconscious during the runs because the only thing on my mind would be the pop waiting for me at the finish. Yes, I said pop, but not just any pop, cream soda. It is funny to think my main motivation at the time was something that in no way aided me after a long run, but in a state minus external competitive expectations, it worked. Modern hydration and recovery science did not exist. It was just me and my pop and I began to take pride in something I did; it settled me, made me feel better about who I was. Each day I would blindly adhere to Bolton's instruction as I did not own a watch, nor did I track mileage. For you youngsters, GPS was reserved for NASA, so we were without guidance. A cream soda and the connection with my sisters, oh, and storytelling, motivated me. I do not know the root of this fascination with telling stories, but this was a gem to share with my classmates: running around a dark park in a relatively questionable area of Chicago logging what seemed to be endless miles. This is where it all began, the humble start of me as a runner.

In time, my abilities began to advance, and I competed at the TAC National Championships in North Carolina with Northview Track Club since Marquette Track Club did not have enough runners my age to field a team. Most would view this season as a sign of my new path in life, but not me. I was part of the national championship team and received my first medal. I don't remember talking about it at all outside of with teammates. It was not transformational; it did not light a fire; it was a medal and a title that had no place in my life. I recall nothing about the event as far as my place or time, it just disappeared, and life resumed.

I was always fast, at least to the degree of my small community of St. John Fisher Parish. The stories of my extracurricular involvement with the club only enhanced the lore. I would run until the sun went down or when someone told me to stop. I never whined or complained, because for some odd reason, this action delivered peace. This feeling of "active rest" continues to this day. Running allows my brain to process and ignites my imagination, unless I am dodging attacks from Redwing Blackbirds which redirects the focus to survival mode. For a child carrying the stress of his own doing, it was the one thing that ultimately tamed me. Running robbed me of my ignorance and put my life at ease. In those moments, I felt more normal and the chaotic mess of my youth would dissipate. My reason for running was unclear. I had no goals so to speak. I did not race to win or achieve a personal record; there was a simple pleasure in just finding a rhythm. It was the purest time of my life from a running perspective. There was no self-induced pressure, I just ran.

It would have made sense that all the positive things that came out of running would lead me to become one. The conflict in grammar school was that I was athletic and played the sport of choice for the season. Life was much simpler back then with limited organized athletic teams. No one ever called each other; there was just a basic understanding. When school dismissed, you went home, changed, and headed to either Monroe Park or Beverly Park. We played football in the fall, basketball in the winter and baseball in the spring. The participant roster was determined based off who showed up. Games would go until sundown and then we would head home for dinner. Time was meaningless; we based everything off daylight.

No matter what we played I was competitive, and it was my outlet. I did not take an interest in girls and school was used as a break between all my activity. Despite my ranging abilities, my classmates tagged me as the fast guy. So, what do you do when recognized for something? With limited confidence in other areas of life, I was left a single option, embrace it, and so I did. I took a lot of pride in this as it was the one thing I could do better than anyone at my school. I was so set on fulfilling this expectation I would even wear my sisters running shoes that were roughly two sizes small since I did not have a pair of my own. They were the only name brand shoes in the house, and I believed they made me look the part. I even accepted the discomfort of my feet going numb mid run. Things, however, began to change, as my friends started to drift into other areas of social interaction.

A few things happened amidst these changes. I retracted to a degree from the social and became consumed primarily with athletics. Enter my Uncle John, conveniently placed as an advocate of an active lifestyle who never shied from an opportunity to teach me something new. He took me on golfing expeditions to Michigan where we would play endless rounds amassing close to 36 holes a day. He introduced me to tennis and anything that did not qualify as one of the big three sports. His forever teacher mentally challenged me in all facets, and I coined him my life coach. John's youth was filled with many athletic accomplishments, but it was time for him to pass the torch to me, the assumed heir.

John's teachings were not limited to the athletic fields. As a master carpenter, we took on a handful of projects together. Despite my want to be "handy," I lacked the natural gift and struggled with patience to do things as meticulously as him. A lot of my dad's brothers acted as mentors in my life; it takes a village, right? John was also a man of stories, so much so, that he compiled a manuscript of his life, far more extensive than this here. He was a man of adventure which many adults questioned, but to me, it was a life I began to envision for myself.

Staying in one place was not a typical attribute of this man. He lived in his van and would take on projects in different parts of the country until complete and then move again. The legend has it he built an entire house himself, but not to live in, he gave it away. This was his nature. When his van magically appeared outside the house along the curb, my energies grew. It was very much like receiving a surprise gift. Staying with us during a project meant he was on the premises, spending nights in his van despite the offering of a room. Material possessions and monetary value were of little relevance to him as whatever he collected, he eventually would seed to his minions. He unloaded his books, technical gadgets, and sporting equipment along with accompanying homework. He did not believe in handouts in the general sense; everything served a purpose.

When is his presence, the one given was that you would learn something. He was a man of action and it was important to him not only to provide as much knowledge as possible to all his nieces and nephews, but keeping the family together was another one of his initiatives. Our family picnics, a highlight of my youth, were a machination of him bringing all of us together to remain connected and young. My strongest recount of these events were the contests he orchestrated, one being a sprint of roughly 100 meters. This became my event, the one I had nerves for and the one I had to win. Even though John exposed me to a wide variety of sports, something was different with running. Maybe it was something intrinsic or even divine, but it reared its head early and popped up many times as I continued to avoid it. After winning the inaugural sprint contest, there appeared to be continual resonation of this running idea no matter how much I tried to bury it. My uncle would have appreciated me going another direction as his aspirations for me were in the realm of golf or tennis.

It was difficult for me once I had left these sports as my relationship with him slowly fell away. I am not sure what the ideal vision for me was in his eyes, but sadly running began to separate us. John suffered from schizophrenia, which as a kid, the symptomatic patterns were unrecognizable; he was just Uncle John. His life revolved around self-sufficiency and a questioning logic of this world. For a time, I followed suit and still do to a degree. John wanted the childlikeness to remain in adulthood, to take the simple joys of activity and not get caught up in meaningless work. When he passed away in 2013, the value of what he contributed to my life became clearer. I see some of him in me, which is one of the greatest gifts he could have bestowed on me. I know in heaven he is probably the head of a social organization that celebrates activity. What he promoted and what he was about, primarily as a teacher of life and its simplicity, continue to challenge me as an adult. Sometimes we move into a new season of life which alters the way we see the world. I would volley back and forth in true relationship with him and I regret that. When we lose someone we love, almost immediately do we wish we had some time back. I miss my uncle but carry his fervor for life with me. It was John's passion that helped me avoid certain temptations that easily would have played havoc on my life.

To Run

Fade Away

The basic understanding of parents in our community was that in grammar school, your children hung out at Monroe Park, and by high school, Beverly Park. I never fell into the behavior of the crowd once drinking and smoking became prevalent. I would show up to compete each night while the rest "hung out", that meant basketball because it was the only illuminated part of the park. As I advanced in years, my visits lessened. I was so fearful of coming home smelling like smoke I eventually pulled the plug on attending at all. Things changed so much that knowledge of my existence evaporated. I occupied this new hermit like state with hoops in the backyard, pitching off the front stairs or mindlessly organizing baseball cards by the team, then the number, then position and on and on. It was my form of hiding, hoping all the challenges the outside world offered would eventually dissipate. In retrospect, it was clear to see that I was one to judge and then dismiss. A lot of friendships fell by the wayside because fear drove me. I did nothing to change the path of anyone but myself, and in doing so, it left me alone. This condition was best summarized by my senior pastor Matt Woodford when he said, "self-absorbed people make self-absorbed decisions". My biggest failure was an inability to see the larger picture. This is common since society puts more emphasis on the "now" which can limit our field of sight. What I was left with was the appearance of righteousness in my mind and conducted the only visits back to the old crew mid run when I would speed past the onlookers at the park.

I often went out on runs at random times with no training plan. The reasoning could have only stemmed from my want of some community or at least being near living human beings. The best runs were when I saw people. Adrenaline would ramp up and my speed would increase. I don't know what my standard pace was, but I would break into a full sprint when running past my peers. Outside of fulfilling the requirement of being the fast kid, I ran scared, always eluding a confrontation of life. When kids wanted to smoke, I ran. When they wanted to drink, I ran. With all else seemingly my weakness, I wanted to harness this slice of good. This was my social life, a mere glance of faceless bodies and then a return to my cavern. I appreciated the simplicity of life although I did not realize that I wasn't living much at all.

I was quick to laugh it off anytime someone challenged me to a race. In gym class, we always had to do some fitness run. I would throw spurts in, turn around, run backwards, mocking the whole ordeal. I feared losing the one thing I thought I was best at. I wrapped all of myself into this single endeavor, which would eventually lead to a fall. This unfortunately came to a head in a science class of all places. We were testing distances using the outside walkway down Fairfield Avenue to conduct our study. At the conclusion, we had races on the officially measured course. What that distance was is still up for debate. The format set two runner's head to head with the runner-up being eliminated. This went on until two runners remained: me and Mickey. Everyone was doing the bragging for me, which allowed me to conceal my fear and remain mute. What I believed to be a sure thing turned into major disappointment; he beat me. As the finish line approached, multiple excuses began to float through my head. I could not recall what they were, but I was very much ashamed. On this day, I saw myself as the ultimate failure and I did what I knew best, I ran from running.

Once I graduated from St. John Fisher, I attended Brother Rice. The thought of running there was not at the top of my priority list. My freshman year I played soccer, basketball and "ran" track & field. Saying I ran track is quite a generous statement considering I was still under the guise I would be the next Michael Jordan or David Justice. For all intents and purposes, it was a place filler. My fall from grace, in relation to running, was quick and my mentality shifted. There were times during soccer practice where we would receive a penalty for a disorganized play or general behavior, resulting in the most severe penalty of all time, to run. The common practice of using running as a form of punishment only made me loathe it more. We were required to run to a tree, roughly 400 meters in distance, and back. You would have thought someone asked us to run a marathon as my dread was that great. I led the disgruntled mumblings as I shuffled back and forth. I wonder where my love of running disappeared, but on those fall days in Chicago, it became an inconvenience.

Basketball was much the same, but when it came down to running commandos or what most refer to as ladders, I was never a slouch. The reminder of my days in grammar school slowly surfaced as I was faced with recognizing some God given talent in running. One day at practice, there were a few extra bodies in the gym rafters: Don Molenda, the head cross-country coach, and Vinnie McAuliffe, the school's top runner. Their purpose became clear when practice let out; they were there to recruit. They pitched the idea about the possibility of joining the track team. I did not have solid spring plans as baseball began to lose its flavor once pitchers learned to throw "junk". Thanks to the success of my cousin Mike, I was a highly touted recruit. The hope was that I had the talent my cousin had. Here they thought they had another Mike Billish.

To Run

I went out for track begrudgingly. The difference this time was that I wasn't competing against a physical competitor, but a ghost in the form of my cousin's success. The first day of practice was a barometer test, where did we stand as far as talent? The required course was a simple out and back from 99th and Pulaski to Western, a four-mile run. These types of runs were common in the city as trails were not easily accessible from the concrete jungle. The grid-system, which is customary in most major cities, makes it very difficult to escape the block by block cycle, although it made tracking distance a simple task. I learned to treasure winding runs once I discovered trails to escape the mental anguish and the doldrums of a city landscape.

Back to the concrete, the run started. I took it out easy and then at about two miles, as my confidence mounted, I felt it out with a surge to no response; I was gone. I finished alone at the front and looked for some validation from the older guys or the coach, but no one was there. I questioned the worth of the torture I just experienced if no one was even there to acknowledge my greatness. This may appear shallow, but I needed something. I needed someone to believe in me because I lacked belief in myself. Either way, I knew that I had to prove myself on another day.

The runs continued as the season progressed, but I fell victim to lagging interest. I skipped practices to go home and play basketball since we just had a new adjustable hoop installed. I deconstructed the former hoop when I had used a steppingstone to launch myself up for a dunk. It was a Shaquille O'Neal moment, but the pure power of the dunk, or the wearing of the old concrete, caused the foundation to erupt from the ground. It was a game over move. The timeout ended with a new hoop that re-birthed my interest. These hoops are common today, but back then, they were the stem of all kinds of creative energy for an athlete who needed a few inches to realize the altitude of a rim rattling dunk. I missed practice often stating some lame excuse. As a coach, these trivial machinations trigger a simple eye roll. I thought no one would catch on to my ploy allowing me to skirt around this unpleasant season. I was mistaken.

As I was finishing a patent Dominique Wilkins' windmill dunk, my father appeared out the back door. Just seeing his figure, twenty feet high off the back porch, casting a shadow from the doorway onto the court, completely shut me down. He asked why I was home and not at practice. The fear in my voice was enough to seal my fate as I alluded to practice being cancelled. This may have been a credible response had it not been 80 degrees without a cloud in the sky. Oh, he also saw the team running on his way home. I was left without response before an ultimatum was issued: "You either try or quit."

This was earth shattering. Never had I been called out before in relation to sport. I was not one to quit, so I decided I would run as the word "quitter" was more damaging than any pain I thought this sport could deliver. My major problem stemmed from the first loss delivered to me in the grammar school science sprint. That made me fear trying because I preferred to not replicate the feeling of pure emptiness. I returned to practice the following day with no miraculous performances, but I was there, fully present. We ended up winning the conference, which was the only time in track that would happen through my time in high school. I was part of the 3200m relay that finished sixth. There was nothing glorious about our placement, but we contributed points to the team total which was gratifying enough. I escaped this season with limited damage and accepted my role as part of a relay. Relays were a "free pass" in my estimation as expectation seemed to split four ways; I appreciated this shelter. At some point I figured this would not be the case which scared me a bit. Whatever would come, would come, but for now, the season was over.

To Run

A Transformational Decision

Before my sophomore season, I had a big decision to make. Was I going to return to soccer or was I going to run cross country? It was the moment I had to address the inevitable. After completing the track season, I had established a bond with my teammates. When I was invited to join them for summer training, I viewed it as an opportunity to speed up my fitness for soccer. With soccer there was little pressure, as no one, at least in my family, had done it before. It was a wide open slate to be what I thought I wanted to be. Cross country would bring back the challenge of being like my cousin. Not only that, my sisters were the top runners at our sister school, Mother McAuley. There were overwhelming mind matters, but my heart knew the rightful path.

I began the cross country summer training without a final decision on which activity would get my time. Even though I was part of the soccer team, one thing was distinctly different in cross country. They welcomed me in a way that had never been the case in my involvement in sports. I'm sure my talent, namesake or the fact that my sisters ran at the largest all girl school in the area which opened some dating chances for my teammates, played into it a little. The feeling was inexplicable with the distance crew. I no longer had to throw out bravado to fit the mold, just being me was enough. The endless reminders of my path continued to come into focus and God's past hints found a home. My resistance lessened as I knew that this was where I belonged. I committed to cross country and my life instantly began to change. I felt freer to be who I was, which was the first time I had met this individual. My reputation as one of the "Bash Brothers" in soccer, as essentially a brute, to a person with greater depth and purpose was an advantage to my reborn passion.

The season began after summer training at Bullfrog Lake and the challenging ten-mile course, but now it was a return to the concrete and grid of yore. As a high school athlete, even in my teaching years, there is something special about the fall, a renewed energy and opportunity to redefine ourselves is always present. This was a time of a rebirth for me, a time to accept who I was. I ran a lot of races that year, primarily at the freshman-sophomore level finishing well, but I had never won. I was still figuring out this new sport and judged my success on this strict guideline to believe I was a distance runner. Something had to give.

To Run

It was a rainy fall day in downtown Chicago at Montrose Harbor alongside Lake Michigan, which played host to the Chicago Catholic League Championships. The course is flat outside of one mound that acts as the centerpiece of the park. The mist played off the lake and leaves littered the ground. The race began as I settled at the front of the pack with the customary sprinters who tested their 200-meter ability from the onset. Despite knowing they would eventually collapse, it had me second guessing. I was nervous, wondering when people would ever fall off, and before I hit the mile, it happened. I was all alone in front of the pack running like an aimless mouse trying to escape capture. I did not understand how to dictate a race which left me with only one option, just run!

I hit the two-mile mark remaining in the lead by a good 200 meters over my teammate and best friend, Ryan. Because of the rain and the leaves that had scattered about the course, it was very difficult to see the poorly decided orange line that marked the direction. I was lost, but fortunately enough for me, the pack followed. I finally found my way after about a 300-meter detour and chaotic yelling from coaches and teammates trying to redirect my path. There was only so far a runner could go off course considering there was a significant obstruction, Lake Michigan. Reconnected with the orange line and back on course, I disappeared under the stone bridge and emerged back into the crowd's vision. This was it, the final stage with just three quarters a mile to go. As I made the final left turn into the finishing straight away, just 400 meters separated me from my first high school victory. An enormous energy roared through me that could not be contained subtly. I pumped my fist and screamed through the shoot, greeted by a teammate, Izzy, who only encouraged further absurdity.

It was exhilarating and was something I had never experienced before. Odd to say, but my prior team national championship paled in comparison. I had won nothing that mattered, but today it mattered. It overwhelmed me with emotion as I turned to see my teammates closely behind. Before I could process my individual crown, another, far greater victory eclipsed it, our team won. It may not have been a state or national title, but it sure felt like it. The team was composed of a group of misfits, longing for a place to belong. Almost our entire team was comprised of those who departed from the soccer or football teams, and now we had finally found our place. This team became my first group of real friends. There was a shared purpose, accountability and support, things foreign to me most of my life.

I quickly replaced my old self-serving ways, and the transformation was immense. I found the benefits of community, and with it I thrived. This group allowed me to step out of the shadows of my past. The transition from my freshman year to my sophomore year could not have contrasted more. My diligence at practice translated into a more focused student, an increase in community involvement, and a greater appreciation for simple things I long took for granted. Running literally changed my life. I no longer questioned if any other sport or activity could have done the same thing. I believe the answer is no; God had a plan. He pulled me and others from different paths and set us on a path together. Life had greater value; I was happier. When we align with God's plan for us, everything has a way of just making sense. The self-conflict I had created by pushing in other directions only led to greater conflict. If everything was a battle, maybe I was fighting in the wrong war or was the reason for these wars. I could not deny it any longer and finally considered myself a runner. There is no other way of explaining the complexity of all things considered. This transition would not have come without the work of a divine being who used my past to redirect my future. The years passed and I broke the tape a handful of times, but I will always remember the moment I stopped fighting myself and let the runner emerge.

There was no better environment for me to discover myself without the culture of a cross country team. Even though I achieved more success on the oval, when all compete on the same course together, the common experience of a team cannot be mimicked. The simple construction of scoring in these events sets the table. A cross country meet requires five runners, possibly six and even seven, to compute a final score. Everyone competes in the same event, making training and competing more streamlined. This lack of variance creates the commonality. It is the sum of all parts and a reason it achieves greater unity. Conversely in track, individuals score in a multitude of disciplines with an expanse of training groups, philosophies and personality. Not limited to scoring, but the chemistry of the team changes as the heterogeneous composite of distance runners are joined by sprinters, throwers, and jumpers. No matter the closeness of the group, something changes with track. The bond from the fall is hard to replicate.

The amount of time spent in the absence of my fellow harriers in high school was seldom. Anything from pre meet hang outs at the Cunningham's, shaved heads to show unity, attended dances and working through the difficulties of life, it was all done together. These men became not only the cheerleaders in my life but psychologists, matchmakers, comedians and protectors. Even though our relationships were not seasonal, a substantial transition came with the new dynamic of track. I quickly accepted the changes as the recognition of my speed, coupled with a limited attention span for distance, filled the void. There was no doubt that the event range matched my specific talents better. With the change in the training program, my confidence surfaced, and I began to view myself more as a track athlete. Over my years in coaching, almost every distance athlete I have coached believed at one point or another that they were made for the bright lights of speed oriented distances. When the dust settled, no Carl Lewis was to be seen. Even though my early experiences were contests of brevity, I didn't think sprinting was my gem, but I knew I was not a two miler either.

To Run

The Fear Factor

When I emerged as a runner in my sophomore year of high school, I figured that all that lay ahead of me was progress. The only problem that made me hesitant was fear. The fear of racing and losing. The fear of being embarrassed in front of teammates and family. In essence, being afraid to be human. Something happens at some stage in our lives that creates these fears as we are not born with them. What shaped me came from lack of unmitigated recognition of my entire person. Athletics was my form of escapism, but that was primarily in association with a team atmosphere. I was no longer protected by the shield of a team once my talent was uncovered; accountability was seemingly mine alone. Losing was not an option in my perfectionistic mind but losing was inevitable. At the freshman-sophomore level, the burden was light, victories compiled, but when I moved up to varsity, there were no guarantees. Our conference had plenty of talent that year and for me to have expected to win every time out was not realistic, but it was the standard I had set for myself. I was never so scared in all my life when I walked to the starting line for the 800 meters at the indoor conference championships. I was the number two seed, although the stretch of me reeling in the top seed was nothing too outlandish. My coaches believed that I could win. This generated pressure which began the downfall of thoughts.

It was the first time that people were expecting good things from me individually. It was a 200-meter track lined on all sides. Whatever happened would not go unnoticed. Before the race, I remember thinking if I was feeling good and with the lead pack, that things would be all right. That thought expired quickly when the crowded field converged at the break line 50 meters in. With the first inkling of pain, my body and thoughts were riveted. I was afraid to feel pain, which would have been enlightening before I committed to a sport with such a high threshold of uncomfortable feeling. I could not see myself losing without a catastrophic incident.

That major glitch in my racing came when I intentionally tripped myself 300 meters into the race to elude the pain and instead assumed shame. That I was willing to accept losing at my own hands shows the sheer power of fear. My thinking at the time was unclear, and I really was not sure what direction that life was taking me. Was I ready to accept losing even if I left everything on the track? Unfortunately, the answer to this question was no. I was not ready to take responsibility for my actions and sacrificed team gain because of personal issues. I had guilt with this performance for some time and vowed to never let it repeat itself otherwise running was not a fit. Even though I don't know how this issue resolved itself, the event was necessary. It is not an alluring story I tell, and it did not come out of me until I coached. It took a certain confidence in myself and the right situation to apply it for the benefit of my athletes. Just like then, eventually I had to move on.

As outdoor conference approached, I went into the 800-meter varsity race as the number four seed. I was more comfortable with this seeding because it made me closer to the role of an underdog than a favorite. I somehow composed myself to do my best, and I limited the pressure put on myself. The expectation slipped a tad after indoors, which allowed me to recover from absolute competitive oblivion. As the race began, I settled at the back of the lead pack in sixth place. We rolled through 400 meters in a meager 61 seconds. Our conference was never known for the 800 meters, so this relatively lax pace was fitting. I always had a kick, and I often used it in my younger, less confident days. 100 meters left, I moved up into third, side by side with second and a short distance behind the leader. With the finish line encroaching, my fear had left me, and I dug deeper than I ever had. With one final push, I pulled it off. I won my first track varsity race, but the larger accomplishment was overcoming the demons from my faulty indoor campaign. The media attention was great, a size four font name and time print in the Chicago Tribune. Fortunately, accolades didn't drive me as I replaced them with the exhilaration of the experience. The result of stepping into an area I didn't feel I belonged before was not only acceptance of my gift, but it lit a fire for competition. It was the largest hurdle I faced, and I began to thrive under this new discovery.

My finish and the advancement of some teammates provided a new opportunity the following week at Sectionals. This was not in my line of sight because of the consumption of my one meet at a time mentality. Our coach decided we would comprise a 3200-meter relay where I was the third leg. The rest of the quartet were all seniors and guys I had looked up to since joining the team a year prior. The weight of expectation was minimal; it was more a shot in the dark than anything. Under the instructions of my coach, I was to play off his cues to determine if the race was a go or not. As I have exercised within my coaching career, you put a questionable leg up front, if they click, game on, but if not, there is time for strategy adjustment. They also entered me in the open 800 where my coach believed there was a more legitimate chance of qualification for the state meet. The open event was more consuming as I wasn't even sure my coach would give me the thumbs up in the relay to race.

Race day came, and we hid ourselves from the oppressive heat under the bleachers for what seemed an endless period which did a number on my psyche. Only to warm up were we allowed to leave our metal cage. When reviewing the race seeds, it did not look good for our crew, especially with the accent of a pure 3200-meter runner on the anchor. My first chance to earn a state birth was now upon me. The gun signaled the start as we quickly dropped behind a mass of competitors. With the exchange, little had changed; it was looking more like I would trot two laps as to not wear myself down for my next race, but something changed. This was not about me; it was about us. The guys who picked me up so many times and supported me deserved a return on their investment.

As they positioned me on the track, far beyond lane one due to the eight teams ahead of us, I watched for my coming teammate. In my head, I knew what the signal would be from my coach, but I overrode it. The baton was slapped into my hand and it was now my turn to take a two lap jaunt. My first quarter mile was faster than prescribed, surpassing the expectation of someone with a lifetime best of 2:01. It turned into a game for me as I retrieved one runner at a time before arriving at the leader. Things changed quickly as the two of us continued to add separation to the weakening field. I did my job, 1:57, a four second improvement and right up front. It was now onto our 3200 specialist. Our confidence was high as he always fought, and in this case, this could have been the end of his career.

The anchor and our shot at state were two laps away. The small lead grew incrementally, but he was hanging and the distance between us and third place did not look as if there was enough real estate for anyone to stage a comeback. In the state of Illinois, if you finished in the top two, you qualified regardless of the time. Our time was not at the official mark, but placement did the job this day. It was the first time I had qualified for the state meet filling me with a swelling confidence. The most telling detail from this race was not that we qualified, which would reaffirm any decision to become a runner, but that I showed up in an important situation. To most it was not even in their field of sight. A year prior, a different story would have resulted, as I am certain I would have adhered to my coach's plan and prepped for my individual event. Something triggered inside of me in those two laps. This could have been all about me, but that thought was not satisfying enough. Three other guys became state qualifiers that day for the first and last time. There was nothing else I wanted then to serve those who served me. We went to state which is pretty much it. The performances were not impressive as we bowed out of preliminaries. Even though our season ended, the memory asserts the fact that I had grown. Change was inevitable with the departure of the senior class, yet it was not the only change. The red track I competed on was being replaced with a new blue surface. I was set on a coming out party the following season to christen the big, blue oval.

To Run

The Curse of the Crowd

I overcame my fear of racing against competition and even to accept pain, but there was one factor that had not erased itself yet, the crowd. Still in its infancy, as there was not much acclaim given to the lower level teams, attention accompanied my movement into the varsity ranks. How would the crowd, my team, and my friends respond to my performances? There was always something I had to work through, and this was next on my list. I was concerned about my appearance as I preferred looking the part over playing the part. I would change my running style, strategy, etc... For some time, I raced for the crowd's approval even if it was self-sabotage. It parallels my life when I was often doing what others wanted me to do for the simple reward of acceptance. It ended up tainting my running. The power of mentality has more to do with your overall scope on life than just that simple moment or activity, and I required validation.

I was a victim, and the mimicking led to losses before a contest had ever taken place. I was influenced based on the fact of who would be in attendance. If there were extra family or friends, especially girlfriends, then I was doomed. I had programmed myself a long while back in grammar school during my competitive basketball days. The stress I put on myself in those situations led to faulty expectations and anger when I could not meet the high demand. I would come off a solid performance only to fold when it mattered, when more bodies were present. If I missed a layup, it was enough to ruin my entire week until the opportunity for redemption arrived. I lived and died many lives through sports because it was where I believed all my talents rested. Go figure that most of my top performances came at low profile events where the pressure was less.

Running may have been my release of stress, but it also started to supply an unhealthy batch. Each race was the end of the world. I had an inability to apply perspective in these formative years and therefore suffered mightily at the hands of something that most of my life provided peace and joy. Running shifted from a dependent life source to a scolding enemy. Every good performance had an expiration date, and even while amidst the celebration of an accomplishment, my energy would shift to the next test. Basically, it did not matter if the performance was good or bad; my mind became occupied either way with another pressure or validating moment. This thinking robbed me of being present and taking in the experience. It was more common to not be able to find me until

To Run

I completed my race. I saw any distraction as a deterrent to accomplishment. I am not sure why my love quickly became my foe. It just proves my ignorance with lacking mastery to temper the outside without pulling it inward. The battle raged within me for years leading into my final high school season.

To Run

When It Rains...

Most seniors approach their final year of high school as a sendoff parade. Some even find frustration when any kind of expectation is placed before them. I relished in this time as I had found my fit and rhythm in many areas of life. With college looming, I wanted to soak in the time left in this community. Despite believing my value in life to be something I did not need reinforced, the fall tested me. I was raised in a tight-knit community and relationships were not limited to the ones within your own school. Many of my St. John Fisher classmates attended other local high schools, but it did not erase the knowledge you possessed of their exploits. Sometimes the distances seemed to grow as everyone became engaged in their new communities, but the relationships were not lost. I was reminded of this early in my year.

There was nothing but hope for the future as I walked in as a senior. I now mastered all things in terms of the school environment, college plans, and social establishment. As the season got underway, a hiccup surfaced. A friend had suffered what doctors communicated as severe dehydration at football practice. He was hospitalized and my first reunion came in the form of a prayer service at my grammar school. Upon my return to the old stomping grounds, my classmates greeted me, despite my errant ways in junior high, and the time was peace filled. We shared our lives with one another and not a moment appeared lost over the past four years. There was a lot of laughter and camaraderie. Our overall demeanor in relationship to the present circumstance was positive. It appeared a divine appointment to return me back to a foundation I had taken for granted.

When we dismissed from this event, life went on as it appeared our friend would make a full recovery. Then the shocking news was delivered. He ran into some complications, and just like that, he was gone. In the infancy of life, I had played witness to loss of family members, primarily my grandparents, but something was different this time. He was my age, a successful athlete, student, and one of the nicest guys I ever knew. It turned my world upside down. The visual of me standing over my desk at home struggling with the question of "why was he chosen" is indelible.

It froze my whole being for a considerable time. When young, we assume that we live life, grow old, and, at some point, pass on. It shook my perspective. How can someone who hasn't even been given the opportunity to live fully be gone? If I ever questioned the meaning of life, this was the most prominent event to date. Continuing the pace of life with all the goals I had was displaced. It removed any selfish thoughts as my heart sank. My desperation was to be around those who knew my friend, but I did not attend the same high school. I returned to school with an inability to focus as life's meaning continually surfaced. My high school offered counselling for those impacted by the loss, but the limited time in those sessions left a full day to take on by myself. Nothing offered solace requiring me to pull away from my active cross country season.

Everything paused and nothing else mattered. The wake and funeral brought together a group I had abandoned years ago with forms of misjudgment as the lives they were living slanted with mine. The budding realization of what I had sacrificed and the openness I witnessed was telling me that these were special people. If I ever questioned God's grace, they cemented it through their expressive forgiveness. What happened during this time was a complete restoration. This group did not judge me; they did not shut me out, but openly embraced me as I had never left. Although there was the loss of one, it brought a large contingent back together. This was God's doing as he provided what we all needed, each other.

Even though it took years for me to wrap my hands around such a catastrophe, my old classmates delivered peace and it gave me the strength to resume life. The only way I could run was by redefining my purpose. I was given a gift, and to honor my lost friend, I needed to use it now, as no day beyond the present was guaranteed. As I emerged repurposed, it replaced any prior stress with meaning. Suffering brought about this change and I discovered things covered from my sight. After a hiatus from life, I returned more impassioned than ever before. Even minus a week of training, my return came with a meet victory and course record. The rest of this year became truly a celebration of life and the blessings put upon me.

When it is stated that it takes a village to aid in any upbringing, my rise resulted from many. Community saved me! Whether it was family, friends (new and old), coaches, or teachers, they gave me a magnificent base of strength and faith to govern my life when in the absence of such support. The clearest detail through my earliest stages of life is that no matter the complexity or difficulty of present circumstance, I was never left minus the grace of God. What He places before us is with intention and our victory over these obstacles is willed when our dependence lies in Him. And so went my senior year, embracing good and bad, but always scouring any circumstance for the silver lining. When my season had not ended the way I envisioned, I returned to my Northview Track Club counterparts for the postseason. Instead of calling it a season, I knew I was not done. A shot at redemption, a silver lining still existed. Although my vision did not extend beyond the regional qualification, a new storyline was being generated. Once I received my bid for nationals, there was no reasoning to continue to race for accolades; it was solely to honor my gift. Different from most races, I was not nervous, doubted nothing, and walked away an All-American.

To Run

Senior Salute

The fall came to a close, but it changed me. It was on to the last semester of high school. I opened myself to this final run and accepted the expectation as a threat in the 800 and 1600 throughout the state. There were some limitations; however, in that the school's scheduling took away the opportunity to race the "big guns". With the competitive level shrinking, I started to race differently. Dependence on someone else to push me in races was not a viable option. This is when I became truly driven. I took every race out from the gun, no longer dependent on a kick. I viewed each race as the only one on the docket contributing to an all-or-nothing mentality. This "gutsy" style, no matter the race, competition or what races were left on my plate, had others, including my coach, viewing this as basic stupidity. What I needed was not to prove to others my rank, but a way to prove to myself that I belonged in the upper echelon of the state. As the post season arrived, I was undefeated in the 800-meter distance and took that to the state preliminaries. Coach Bill Gleeson believed from the get-go, reminding me often, that it was my time to get a shot at the infamous Marius Bakken. With qualifying in both the 800 and 1600, I decided to scratch the 1600 to take away any distraction or unneeded leg ware. An additional sacrifice was skipping out on graduation celebrations to make my trip to Charleston, Illinois and Eastern Illinois University, the home of the state championships even to this day.

All distractions needed to go and instead of staying in the dormitories that caused stress in the year's past, I opted to stay with my parents at a bed-and-breakfast on the edge of town. There was one aim, get to finals! We showed up to the track on Friday afternoon for the 800 preliminaries. I knew there was work to be done as an All-State nod could only come with advancement. I was the number one seed in my heat and started in lane one, position one. The gun quickly blasted as the announcer came over the loudspeaker announcing the final 800-meter section. The advantage of this heat was that we knew what needed to be run to advance to finals. Despite this additional knowledge, it was of no consequence to me as splits were not part of how I raced. Over time, I had learned to read my body well enough. I knew what a 1:54 felt like and that is what I relied on.

I went out a little more conservative than usual, but the field mended from the start to 400 meters crossing the line almost in unison at 57 seconds. There was very little jostling for position, the symmetry of running's beauty. It was as if each athlete was in their own race. I sat in eighth place through halfway and then started to bridge the gap to the front. Each person I captured propelled me to the next and the endless stream of competitors slowly slipped behind me. I began to move into the top five. I went from fourth to third with 300 meters remaining. At 150 meters, I was now sitting in second and gaining. The angelic voice of Matt Piescinski came over the public address informing the crowd of my movement into second place referring to me as "Brother Rice". The final straightaway was all that lied ahead now, and it was a two-man race. The kick I had left behind earlier in the season now returned. The announcer juggled names, "It's Brother Rice and Geneva, Brother Rice and Geneva, oh, very close." I was going to finals after winning my heat and the day's work complete. We limited time on campus and quickly retreated to the bed-and-breakfast. The escape from the environment was probably a blessing. It provided an opportunity to stay away from overconsumption. It was work like, show up to work, do your job and head home before returning the following day. The only catch here was it was about to be my last day of employment in a Brother Rice suit. The next day I would face the highly favored Marius Bakken of York who was attempting to pull off the triple (win the 3200, 800, and 1600). I had an opportunity to play disruptor. Multiple destinies all converged on that final day.

Saturday came and Marius had begun his journey easily pulling off a 3200 win, but mine had yet to start. I headed to the check in tent, which acts as the threshold between showing up and competing. As each athlete enters, they cut all the supporters and coaches off and the athlete is now on their own. The tension of the athletes was palpable. There were rows of folding chairs and I positioned myself in the back, far away from any other competitor. From there, I was alone with myself in the company of other athletes equally alone. I sat there contemplating the journey that brought me there. Qualifying took the nerves right out of me.

There was nothing left to qualify for, it was the final race of the season. All I had to do was show up and run. They made the call for us to exit the tent and enter the track. It was like sitting outside the principal's office when your name is called and finally, it was time to enter. What was to come was beyond my understanding. The magnitude of this moment was great; it was the last time I would race as a high school athlete. The crowd was enormous and the main grandstand at Eastern Illinois was at capacity. I could not wait to be "released" which is the time they grant the athletes freedom to stride out into the awaiting masses. I felt like everybody was watching me, wishing they could be a part of it; I was part of it!

I stood at the line for what seemed to be hours as the heat intensified, and the announcer diverted to the award stand. The most amazing part of this is that there were thousands of people, a handful of athletes, and utter silence. After the award presentation was complete, they introduced the field. Once the stage was set, the gun finally broke in. I used the same strategy from the previous day and sat with the caboose of the pack using the entire back straightaway to move into the inside lanes from my alley four starting position. From an onlooker's perspective, with the quality of the field, my season would appear to be at an end; there was no way I could overcome the lead that quickly developed. Through 400 meters, the pack once again converged as it had the day before. The entire field checked through the 400 at 56 seconds, but then the moves came. I remember thinking as I was making the turn 500 meters in that I was in sixth, "I am All-State right now", but this thought did not limit me to being satisfied, it pulled any remaining doubt... I had a safety; it was time to go.

As we galloped down the backstretch, I continued to pick guys off. With 200 meters to go, I moved into fourth as we strung out in a line. The moment brainwashed me, and I defaulted to the most routine thing I knew, let the legs just go. In the final straightaway as my dad prayed aloud saying "get third, get third", the announcer erupted, "Marius Bakken in second, Dan Billish of Brother Rice in third". It was done, an All-State ending, and a school record. It was a moment I had envisioned through countless miles and workouts when I would create images of where I wanted to be. Legendary York High School coach Joe Newton often referred to this race as the best race he had ever seen. Much of that acclaim resulted from how Marius fought, but a nice compliment from a man I am certain saw some remarkable things. The storyline continues to replay itself in vivid detail, but the actual event was a wink.

Although a goal of mine was realized, it did not share the same exuberance as my first cross country win, but I could not contain my smile. I was more for savoring the experience. My entire high school journey culminated in that moment without bravado, but peace. I returned to the check-in tent to gather my things before awards and the intimidation of this place was lost. I sought my family and friends who supported me, exchanged hugs and handshakes, but one thing was missing, my dad. As he approached with video camera wobbling in hand, my eyes began to tear. "We did it" I uttered. We hugged and the moment still comforts me to this day.

Running is the soundtrack of my life. There is a VHS cassette somewhere in the depths of my basement, and despite its format being out of popular usage, the taping of the state championships my senior year is something I hold on to in my mind and heart. My dad videotaped every race I ran, albeit, some fidgety or showered over with his interior monologue making its way to the public ear. From the video, I heard my dad say "he's cooking" with 200 meters to go. As I came into the final straightaway, my mother's tearful cries of "go Dan" echo. When the finish line eclipsed, my dad mumbled, "Way to go to bud." That was my day; that was our day. In watching that race over and over, my memory has been usurped by the love I heard from my parents' responses and engagement. It was pure; it was love. It is the most poignant memory that goes far beyond the running realm. I guess running did something for me. My parents were "all in" on my life, and this shared moment was a victory that far superseded the track. I know that the outcome of this event and many others were because of my father's brutal honesty and challenge. Without his call to action, I would have never been in the position I was; it shaped me. What was to come directly resulted from my parents' council.

To Run

Final Exam

My high school experience marked the evolution of a child to man. With this growth, I sought a community that would continue this progress. In my college decision, I decided on a major out of necessity rather than want. A big component of sorting through opportunities was running. Without the Internet to take virtual tours and explore every detail the school offered, I had resorted to recruitment letters. The other avenue to gather knowledge on these schools came in the form of information folders. I still question my options had I not been an athlete. I did not explore a single school that did not recruit me. Although I became excited with each new letter that arrived, I knew that I would not be travelling too far from home, which eliminated Columbia University in New York. My final choices came down to Indiana University, University of Wisconsin, and Loyola University. Each school had something unique to offer, and all would entertain my dream of running in college. Two of the schools had an unfair advantage from the onset based on my fandom of athletes who attended those schools.

This was not a time where distance runners were glamorized in society, even to the specific running community. I did have knowledge of a few though and held on to newspaper articles about Jim Westphal, a former Illinois 3200-meter state champion, multiple time All-American at Loyola University and a member of the United States World Cross Country team. The other member of my limited "Wall of Fame" was Bob Kennedy, arguably the best American distance runner of all time and the first non-African to dip under 13 minutes in the 5000 meters. His career at Indiana University was nothing short of stellar. Both were still training under their former college coaches, which added additional intrigue. I looked up to both and was even starry-eyed when I met Jim at my cousin's college graduation party since they were teammates at Loyola. Jim now coaches locally at Hinsdale Central High School. I have reminded him of his fame from yesteryear although that has been replaced with many high school successes. He found it far-fetched that he had a fan, but that is a simple attribute of his humble nature. Bob was more elusive and my opportunity to meet him was still incomplete.

As I evaluated programs, one thing continued to rear its head in, money: the word that uproots dreams. So many athletes become consumed by this idea that they make decisions that are not pure. Do you have a full ride? How much are you getting? These questions often create a disconnect in a high school student's brain. Does one sound more successful if they say they are going to college on a full ride? Possibly, but I was thankful for my parents to allow me to feel out my new home and take away any fear regarding money. This was a time in my life I charted new territory. Both of my sisters were Division I athletes, and both were on full rides. I had opportunities to join them at their respective programs, but I was looking for a new experience, escape the shadows, and forge my path. I thought the only way for me to be myself was to get as far away as possible, but not too far. All my friends were looking to attend schools in Illinois, which made the decision to move out of state more difficult. Despite this roadblock, I was being called in a new direction. I did not want to leave my friends, but I had to leave my friends. I needed a chance to find myself at an even deeper level without expectations of past standards. This was the first step I took in finding out exactly who I was.

I visited all my final choices, but the decision became simple after I arrived in Bloomington. My dad and I were greeted by Sam Bell and Marshall Goss, two Indiana legends. The weather could not have been worse, cold with a continuous rain, so seeing the campus through windshield wipers was not ideal. We raced through the Indiana campus in Coach Bell's blue Subaru Outback. His aggressive driving demeanor spoke volumes about what his intensity as a coach would look like. The familiar sighting of this car is stained in my memory as it guided many of our workouts when not on the cross country course.

On other visits, I was more occupied with the athletes than the coaches, but this was very much the opposite. It was clear from the beginning that these two men, who mimicked father figures, had genuine care for their athletes. They were stern but going back to Coaches Bolton, Molenda, and Gleeson, this command benefited me in the past. As a young man seeking discipline, it naturally fit. This was an era where great coaches not only cared for their athletes, but accommodation was not common. I required discipline, and I was far from being a running savant. In attending Indiana (IU), there was a slew of legendary coaches that expected a high degree of discipline, men I admired for their integrity. Sam Bell and Marshall Goss were right alongside Bobby Knight, James Counsilman, Jerry Yeagley, and Bill Mallory. This is what I signed up for and it is what I wanted to receive.

Throughout my visit, I did not meet a single member of the team, but I saw something that stuck in my mind. While Coach Bell recklessly cruised the campus, I noticed someone running quickly, adorned with two air casts on his lower legs. It was the clearest image that remains now some years later and a signature divine intercession. He, running on his own, on a rainy, cold day with obvious lower leg issues spoke of sacrifice and leadership. He was my guide throughout the early years. Matt Sparks, a senior on the team, became a mentor, coach, and friend. Matt is the head coach at The University of Notre Dame, and the fact he is there and having the success he is, does not surprise me in the least. They sold me without a word spoken to a team member while parading around a saturated campus because I felt comfortable entrusting my career and future to the men sitting in front of me. I was not one of their top tier recruits by any means, but I sure felt like it. I could not be more thankful for these men and them embracing me into their family.

On the return home, there was no doubt that I would attend Indiana University in Bloomington, Indiana. The one reason that I was hesitant in stating my final decision was because I was nervous about putting too much financial burden on my parents. My sisters left no imprint of debt on them and were even aided through their graduate studies. I had this opportunity, but not in Bloomington, where I believed I was destined to be. It was then my dad reassured me of my decision. He told me to not worry about the money, and to go where you believe you will be happiest. The decision was final.

My last summer was one I will never forget. I would be an Indiana Hoosier and run for the legendary Sam Bell. My friends were all happy for me but would continue to hamper me about scholarships. I was always a little shy on the subject and would often veer the conservation in another direction. I was getting the chance to do something that was uncommon in my community. It was always about worth; how much was a school willing to put up to have me on their team? The school selection was less stressful than the money situation, but that quickly dissipated as I began to focus more on my arrival in Bloomington for fall training. The last weeks of summer were difficult ones. I had to say goodbye to the first real friends I had ever had to venture into a world that was virtually unknown. It was a rite of passage toward independence. With all the newness, the only thing that helped restore my confidence about my decision was running.

PART TWO
Summer

To Run

Starting Over

I met with the team and instantly felt out of place. Most of the
guys were natives of Indiana and had many stories to share about
competing against one another in high school. There was one other
from Illinois, but he was confined within himself. I listened to the
dialogue with limited interplay as I fell into the mold of shyness,
resulting in discomfort. It probably worked out better for me since
I couldn't speak much during the runs anyway based on simple
exasperation. The training regimen ratcheted up considerably from
my experiences. Bell's plan implemented both high mileage,
including doubles, and high intensity, not to mention time was
extremely relevant in terms of pace. It was a long year for all of us
freshman. The other change I had to make was being away from
home. I had a roommate from my high school who I was relatively
good friends with, unfortunately, the life of a regular college student
versus an athlete found little common ground.

Each day was a struggle as we had double runs with a morning run
at 6:15 and our main workout at 3:00. I had never doubled outside

of my visit to the University of Wisconsin Camp of Champions where there were no other things to balance, and the visit was short enough that homesickness was a nonfactor. Tack on required visits to the training room pre and post workout and academic training tables each evening resulting in a full slate of personal freedom sacrifice. To complicate matters, the freshman had not learned how to pace themselves. I recall some peers blasting out in the morning, something frowned upon by the upperclassmen. The response to such an egregious act was clear. By the time our main workout in the afternoon would roll around, these "fresh fish" were defeated from the morning's run. Gentle pace was close to six minute miles. I had never gone on a supposed gentle run with a coach in tow who continually read off splits. As a newcomer, the dichotomy between coach and teammate pleasing was difficult to balance, especially since I had a lot to prove.

The U.S. Track & Field and Cross Country Coaches Association (USTFCCCA) ranked our freshman class as a top three recruiting class in the nation, so the pedigree was impressive. We had state champions from Indiana, California, Michigan, and Missouri. Whatever past credentials, they did not matter since everyone yielded an equally legitimate resume. One little glitch was enough to drop from the talent of this group. Every run was hard labor, not only physically but mentally, with an inability to escape the clock. Most of the freshmen did not recover from the stressful load and quickly our top recruits were done for the season with injuries that continued to plague them all year. I guess there was an advantage to growing up in Chicago with no training facilities outside of a weeded old cinder track and pounding on pavement. This once inconvenience helped me develop an uncanny tolerance to impact stress. A lot of our training loops were on roads when we were not being challenged by our permanent, hilly cross country course. This might have upset me more as our team withered, but with lacking development of relationships, every person was competition. Beyond that, it created an opportunity to make the cross country roster.

When I was recruited, my primary role was predestined for track and field, an afterthought for cross country. I chose to not wait for track season to show my abilities, instead; I put my head down and chucked all my energies into this singular endeavor. Coach Bell had little knowledge of my past cross country exploits primarily a result of the Illinois distances being inconsistent creating an obstacle in recruiting cross country runners from the state. This was prior to the establishment of the Nike Cross Country Nationals (NXR, NXN) and limited participation in Footlocker regionals. The popularity of these circuits helped exercise consistency from state to state with more head-to-head competition and mirrored distances. The Internet was just being born so the oval was the primary fitness tracker and the reason for my predicament. Overall, exposure was limited. I always ran with a chip on my shoulder and this provided me with even more motivation to prove that I belonged there. My option to create a cross country runner's profile began at what Bell referred to as the Barbeque Run, which marked the beginning of each season. For most of the elders, this was a simple tempo workout, but it was also the event that would fill out the roster. This was a day for all the "plebeians" to make a name for themselves. Returning varsity runners were all adorned in their school issued gear while the rest of us, typically shirtless, racing for the opportunity to join the uniformed. I hoped that I would shed my blue Nike kit at the completion of this contest.

The Meaning Behind a Uniform

As another race day approached, the thought of competing always triggered my emotion and nostalgia of all that was done to put me in the place I stood. Outside of the motivation of a team and goals, there was one item that was transformative as a runner, the uniform. When I ran before my high school years, there was really no unveiling come race day. I wore the only running shoes I owned, whatever shorts were clean and a long sleeve, black Northview Track Club tee shirt. Part of this slipshod outfitting had a lot to do with lacking knowledge of the program's history and my aimless purpose. I am sure that some kids on the team understood what it meant to wear that uniform, but I was an ignorant one. It was just another shirt.

When I arrived at high school, things changed. It now mattered in my eyes; it was relevant. Brother Rice was not known as a state contender in cross country or track & field, but that did not erase the magic when adorning the uniform. The knowledge of my cousin's accomplishments and it being my father's alma mater gave it meaning. A uniform reflects not only what school or team you are associated with, it marks a journey that started a long time ago. It is part of the goals and dreams we have and what we hope to accomplish. The day we finally put on that uniform marks a met goal and beginning of future aspirations.

In high school, the moments leading up to race time were full of anticipation, the time we would reveal our new armor. Each year, as the team took form together, we came up with tokens to remind us of the shared commitment we were running for. One year we wore black Nike socks, another, a singular wrist band. The meaning finally came to me my senior year. These wristbands were a visible testament of the years of battles, developed friendships, culminating in our final season to stand as one. Times were about to change, but what we had built would carry on. Other people would look at the wristband as an accessory, but it was a solemn unspoken oath taken by each guy on our team. It was not only a reminder, but an honor. I felt privileged to put on that uniform. By the end of my years, my uniform identified me. Names became common for the more established runners, but that didn't mean that people would recognize them out on the street. It required the banner to bring things full circle. The Brother Rice jersey spoke my name, and I was proud of this association. Even today, as a coach, when I see certain uniforms, certain teams and individuals from the past come to mind. The uniform acts as a legacy. It tells the story of the past and all those who contributed to it.

In college there was a new pride. I was now part of an exclusive group. It took many years for me to have the opportunity to continue my career as an Indiana Hoosier. I would have to earn this recognition and the opportunity to sport the red, white, and blue jersey made meaningful by one of my heroes, Bob Kennedy. This was the last jersey he wore his senior year when he took home the NCAA cross country crown. There was nothing I wanted more than to join this esteemed company. I was consumed with many grandiose thoughts all leading up to the "on your marks, go!" command.

The race began and all the minutia fell away. As I slipped behind the returning varsity athletes, every obstacle, minus the actual runners, brought pain to the forefront. Even though the course was on grass, the worn paths contributed to rising dust from each step and a chalky film coating my mouth. There was never a time in my life when I felt so much pain running on the hills of the IU cross country course. A brief reminder, I was from the south side of Chicago where the only hill was an old toboggan stairway at Swallow Cliff, part of the Cook County Forest Preserve. Along with the training that was taking all my energy, I was having problems sleeping. The primary recovery drug was in deficit which only heightened my emotional instability. Doubt was the result, and like any endeavor, there is a threshold. I did not know if I would make it past this one. My freshman year I may have averaged four to five hours of sleep a night with most of that sleep being interrupted to a degree. Most days I would return from morning runs to sneak in an extra 30-minute nap before heading to class. Sleep was my number one concern and that along with my homesickness did not aid the academic burdens I was facing. There were nights when I was so tired that if the phone would ring or our door open, I would automatically get up and dress for practice and ready myself for the trek to Assembly Hall. My roommate would look at me as if I was crazy and say, "Where are you going, it's 3 a.m.?" At this point, I would mechanically crawl back into bed and sleep the remaining two hours before I would rise again.

Despite the gravity of these ailments, my singular focus returned to making the team's roster even though the demons were doing a number on my confidence. As the race continued, I began to pass red jersey after red jersey until I arrived in the top ten. With this continual upward movement, the summit looked more and more attainable. The final kilometer was the most challenging but fortunately I came alongside another freshman, Nate Jones and his brother Matt, who fed me encouragement and carried me through to the finish. I somehow pulled it off and had made the roster and secured the coveted uniform! The feeling of accomplishing this goal far surpassed my physical weakness. I could not wait to get back to my dormitory room to call my parents with the news. I knew that I had accomplished something, and I wanted everyone at home to know that I was doing just fine, when, it was far from the truth.

To Run

Stay or Go?

The intensive workload tangled with insomnia began to catch up with me, which made staying awake in class difficult and recovery near an impossibility. Whenever I become overtired, I have a problem controlling my emotions. The result was a heavy doubt in my current positioning. This was the time of trial I went through trying to figure out if Indiana was the place for me. I missed my friends from home and struggled with any level of social life due to exhaustion. Every free moment was an opportunity to sleep and nothing else. I was presented with the opportunity to run again, this time back to Chicago to attend Loyola University. It was the quintessential grass is greener mentality and I was set on this being the outcome and solution for my problems. Even without making a freak move with a short sample size of experience, I guess I valued comfort in moving back home. Knowing that this option existed helped me get through the rough days. It became my get out of jail free card. I wanted to leave, but that conflicted with the pride associated with leaving. I may not have been pleased with my current situation, but it offset some feelings of failure if I were to uproot from Bloomington.

To Run

As I set some of these complications on the back burner, the team began to spend more time together outside of practice from meals at McNutt Quad, road trips to each other's hometowns, and the shared experience of our struggles. This provided an opportunity to confide in others, yet a burden remained. We came in with high expectations placed upon us, but things were not materializing. A lot of injuries, burnout, exhaustion and social preoccupations began a slow fade of promise. The drive to run was a challenge as my fitness stagnated. I began to seek excuses to escape the struggles that existed within me. I did not read my body because I thought it was a weakness. I would rather act like I was fine and could handle the load even if it was wiping me out and disrupting the quality of my life. I viewed rest as a cursory, something that depleted all the valued stock. Sometimes we need to neglect our thresholds to expand our boundaries, but this was not the case in my situation.

Indoor came, and I won my first race. You could say it was a gift from teammate Chris Ekman who took a nasty spill one lap into the 800 which left me in front by 30 meters. I was hardly conscious what took place, but somehow seamlessly made it through the chaos. It was almost as if I blinked sitting mid pack and when my eyes opened, I was in space. The question rattled in my brain, "When are they going to catch me?" Once the bell rang on the final lap, I redirected my thoughts and I felt just like I did in high school. I ran a mediocre time based on college standards, but the win provided some hope I would rise again.

The rest of the season came with increasing stress, a result of the tank being empty. Nevertheless, I was selected to run at the Big Ten Championships, a great honor for a freshman. Trial by fire, as they commonly say it, was the course of my lead off leg in the distance medley relay or DMR (1200, 400, 800, 1600). I had never run a 1200 and the subsequent time of my leg was telling, a meager 3:09, just a hair out of last. The next two continued my rhythm, slow leg after slow leg until the baton was passed to senior captain, Matt Sparks. At this point we were so far out of the race it almost seemed logical for him to hold back and save for the 5000-meter final scheduled for the following day. The three of us were ashamed of what just transpired and did not question that Matt deserved a free pass. Coach Bell did not see the logic and became enraged with his fifth-year senior sandbagging a championship race. I don't know how long this impression lasted, but Bell noted to the team afterwards it "was the worst individual competitive effort" that he had ever seen. I still feel bad to this day for Matt having to line up with a handful of clueless freshmen as we all felt undeserving of being lined up with him in the first place. Either way, this marked the end of my competitive running for my freshman campaign.

Outdoor quickly approached and with my academics in the shape they were and an inability to switch tempo, I sidelined the season and claimed my first red shirt. I was always a good student, so my struggles in this department were shocking, more so, embarrassing. At the request of the athletic department, they called me to attend an academic meeting at the Indiana Memorial Union. I spoke no word of this to teammates, and I would have preferred to walk into this meeting with a hoodie and sunglasses on to protect my identity. When I arrived at the massive hall to see the place was practically full, a little comfort came over me, but then came the shouting, "Billish" followed by an eruption of laughter. As I glanced to my right, I saw practically the entire freshman cross country class. The shameful feelings started to disband; I was not alone in this transition. This instance began a bond with my teammates that never ceased. I had nothing to hide from them; I could hit a snag and still be myself.

Now part of a shared struggle, leaving Indiana was off the chop block. I made some good friends, figured out the system to a degree, both training and academic, and IU quickly became home. With the drop in intensity, as my focus transferred to cross country preparation, I was able to better manage my sleep and schoolwork. It was the break I needed to understand that my viewpoint of my experience was result of the shadow cast on me when my body and mind were in depletion. Further encouragement of my fit was when

Tom Chorny, a teammate I did not communicate with much at the time and knew primarily for his futuristic hairstyles, reached out to see if I would like to live with him and some guys the following year. I am not sure why I was on that selection list, but it created a new excitement, dormitory life was no more! My address for the rest of my college days would be 202 E. 16th St. Besides Tom, now the head coach at Miami University, I joined Jon Teipen, a transfer from Ball State, Jon's brother, Jeremy, and Aaron Gillen, former California State Champion. Something excited me for the change and figured living with more like-minded people would serve me well.

I returned home to Chicago that summer and worked for my dad at his roofing/contracting company. It was a plush job in retrospect as my father was incredibly flexible around my running schedule. I was a very lazy person outside of running and anything that seemed to tamper with my energy levels would cause me to retreat from whatever endeavor would dare attempt to rob me of that vital energy. I believed that if I was going to be a good runner, then I would have to make certain sacrifices and one of the most logical sacrifices would be extraneous work. My drive for running began to resurface as my confidence mounted from now being a veteran with much needed rest from the rigors of my freshman year.

To Run

New Fire

A staple in our family was competing in the Ridge Run 5K/10K every year. In high school, this was always the weekend of the state meet, but it was a given we would all run or at least walk it. In past years, I just hung out as I was still recovering from the mental toil of a season. Despite my red shirt season, I was still building strength and mileage the entire spring. I began the race without necessarily a goal in mind, but I found myself in the lead pack. It was a new feeling for me. Not only did I feel strong, but I had a new ability. I threw in surges and felt completely in control. This was a far cry from just a year prior. Something had changed; I knew I would be a different beast come the fall. Besides my confident training, it surprised me when word came down that Marius Bakken, one of the best runners in Illinois history, had chosen to attend IU after a year in Norway. The intrigue was great as one of my competitors and someone familiar with my state lingo would now be a teammate. There were a handful of York Dukes on the team due to the pipeline established well before my time between Joe Newton and Sam Bell. Newton always saw Bell as a mentor, so it was not a surprise when Joe walked into our locker room my freshman year. Without me speaking a word, he rattled off all my high school accolades and said, in his way, "Hey Danny, how's my friend treating you?" I had a great respect for this man even though he had never coached me and cherished the relationship developed in my adult years. After hearing word of my new teammate, the dots started to connect that this visit was to cement some details of the transaction to bring Marius to Bloomington.

My summer training went well even though I had to sacrifice a lot of time with my friends to prepare for runs. My friends never really understood my passion for running, or maybe I just did not understand the inner workings of friendship. It is sad to say, but the blinders began to unthread some of those friendships because I was holding so close to this dream. The one positive was that my best friend also ran in college. Ryan Butler ran for the Division III powerhouse North Central College. His remarkable story has been one I have shared with those I teach and coach. School was not the best fit for him, but he made do. In his years of torment because of his involvement with a lower tier academic program at our high school, he continued to press on. Most would have assumed that he would be off to trade school or no schooling at all, but I am sure deep down, he tucked away these limited expectations and used them to fuel his desire to be a police officer. He attended North Central and thrived. Not only was he where society believed he did not belong, he elevated his academic growth, ran for the legendary

Al Carius, and his goal was eventually realized. Despite the challenge of an accident his junior year which left him with a broken hip and out of school, he made up the classes in the summer and was afforded the chance to add a class to each trimester to graduate on time. He left with a degree in sociology and joined the force soon after. In Ryan, I always had a training partner, although he had a "real job" which consumed much of his time. He was the one from my high school friend pool who believed in me and what I was doing. Even though we don't talk as much as I would like, I still hold a tremendous amount of respect and love for this Chicago Policeman.

To Run

Fresh Perspective

It was now time to return to IU for the fall cross country season. I could handle the workouts like I did in high school allowing me to not just survive but challenge myself. I was keeping up with my roommate, Aaron Gillen, who was our present number one. Things were clicking and I had the luxury of being one of the uniformed at the Barbeque Run. I began the season as our number three running faster than I had run at the end of the previous year. I thought it was the best thing in the world until reality unfolded the plight of the Indiana program. I never wanted to be a number for number sake. Sure, it sounded good if you enjoyed being a national doormat?

The entire year, I ran as the team's third or fourth man contributing to abysmal team results. For the first time in over ten years, we lost the Big State Championship, also known as Indiana Intercollegiate. This is the race that includes all the schools from Indiana. The only team that should have offered any competition

97

was Notre Dame, but they didn't even show. We were a wreck and ended up finishing the season in eighth place at the Big Ten Championships to join our tenth place finish at the Great Lakes Regional. Outside of Marius Bakken's qualification for NCAA's and his 28th place performance, the season was a wash. With indoors, I found more value in my performances. This was the beginning of my relationship with training philosophy. As I continued the analysis of Bell's gentle, swing, and crisp language, it began to tangle with another voice, Marius Bakken and Peter Coe.

Marius (Doc Bak) was wise beyond his years and not surprising he became a two time Olympian and medical doctor. Outside his obsession with candy, he measured and analyzed everything in a way I had never experienced. We traveled often together since quick weekend stints home (Elmhurst for Marius) were near one another and I had a car. The transformation of that year defined me a lot of ways as a runner and ultimately as a coach. No longer would I simply run what I was told to run without a second thought; I wanted to understand the purposes of each mile logged. The four hour commute home and back became a hotbed of knowledge sharing. He began as a high school competitor of mine and became more of a teacher in our time at IU together and my appreciation for him only grew.

During a trip home for one of our breaks, Marius had rummaged into some old newspaper clippings and a scrapbook of my senior season. As he turned the pages, I was curious what was drawing his attention. He was on the state cross country page where there was a picture of my friend Matt Macievic, the 1995 cross country, state champion, which noted, "Matt sends Marius on a plane back to Norway". Marius delivered a swift punch to my shoulder as he finished reading that line. This opened the door to a conversation about his transplant to Illinois his senior year. He shared the conversations prior to the track & field state meet and the concerns that him and Coach Newton had of who could block his potential triple. It was me. The fact that I was running times without competition made them leery what I could do with other bodies pushing me. It was a humbling moment for certain, but it went beyond racing itself. I was part of the Marius resistance movement and my ignorance became clearer to me in that moment.

As an athlete who had worked so hard to get where I was, and other competitors of mine, it frustrated us that our senior years were to be tarnished by an imposter. All the attention went to this York Phenom, all the while the spotlight receded on us. To say that ego was not at the root of our frustrations would be false. How often in life do we pigeonhole people based on circumstance or more so, on someone who takes some of, what we believe to be, our attention? What I can be thankful for is that I got to know Marius as a person and dispel my past, polluted thoughts. No matter the talent or societal position, at the end of the day, all are human and all face battles. My assumption that Marius was intentionally showing up to rain on my parade is a ridiculous thought now. He had the pressure put on him by simple placement in a community that lived and breathed running. His shift took a great deal of courage and I commend him for it. Marius was just another teenager with dreams, and shockingly, insecurities. It made me question myself to have an awareness of circumstances outside of another's control. It would have been a shame if I never got to know Marius as his contributions in my life changed my attitude as an athlete, coach, and person.

With the additional guidance, what happened was a drop in my lifetime 800 PR, with wins at the Indiana Invitational and Indiana USATFs. This new perspective was soon to be tested at the Big Ten Championships where the year before, my dismal performance put Sparks in a tough spot, and coach Bell quote lore. I was again slated to run the DMR, but this year I would run the 800 leg. Another year under my belt running my preferred distance was a bonus, and closer to home at Purdue University in West Lafayette, Indiana. Running for a Big Ten school had its advantages for sure, but it was seldom that I ran anywhere close to home. Just a few short hours from Chicago meant a home crowd. This added perk along with my emboldened race approach left a repeat performance out of the question. After the first two exchanges, we sat in fifth as the baton entered my hand. I jolted to the main pack and settled in through 400 meters before putting a surge on Wisconsin and Michigan and ended my leg in third with a solid split. These "mental wins" created the image of fitting in as a Big Ten athlete, that I belonged where I was and could accomplish even bigger feats. My outdoor season ended with substantial drops in time and another PR at the USTCA's leaving me with a lot more to bring into my summer training. A far cry from the previous year with little need to reboot. I was under the belief that I finally assimilated to the college scene.

In addition, throughout my first few years, I had opportunities few would dream of, probably because they were distance runner dreams. One of the fastest distance runners of all time would pop in here and there for workouts. The legendary Bob Kennedy took on some Woodcrest miles with us and some track work. They recruited Mikko and me one day when Bob was looking to knock out some speed. The task was to accompany him through some 150 meter sets. Coach Bell instructed us to push the pace putting us near top speed. Who was I to be running with this guy? It was a fond memory for sure, saddling alongside my hero. Over time, I watched him run insane mile repeats, each one far beyond my lifetime best, and his dance with quarters, 60 & 60: 60 second quarter with 60 second rest which went on endlessly. Watching this man and his intensity in the flesh made it clear why he was one of the best. One thing I found captivating was when he would strap on the shoes with his own namesake attached: the "Zoom Kennedy." It was like watching Michael Jordan tug on the shoes that enveloped a generation. Although I idolized Bob and Jim Westphal as athletes, their status beyond running only upgraded in time. Both are phenomenal men who were not only good at what they did but are as good as what they do now. I picked two fine models for certain and I wanted to thank them for the continued inspiration that drove me back in high school and beyond.

My New Family

Running was clicking and what offered even greater comfort was that the team began to mesh extremely well. Pretty much every part of my day included at least one of my teammates, not to mention that I lived in a duplex with four of them connected to five others. Everything we did was an adventure. A common thread post workout was getting in some light miles on the well-manicured infield of the track. We often would run barefoot, especially on this occasion, considering Bloomington had been doused with rain and there was no reason to soak our trainers as we retired our spikes from the workout anyhow. As we ran our laps, the surface spit in response to our legs pounding. There had been a shadow over this town for some days and we were just happy that the rain had stopped.

My entrepreneurial spirit saw an opportunity unfold. Why not take advantage of this giant slip and slide in front of us? As we approached the main straight, I surged past the group and slid on the grass as a baseball player would take on a base, rhythmically returning to my feet right with the pack. Eyes began to glisten with curiosity as my slide covered a good 20 feet of distance. Many repeated the conventional slide, but then things were elevated as style points became a must. As we felt alive and in our own world, the rest of the track team questioned our sanity resulting in no change. The circus act continued, and Gillen was next man up. As he dove headfirst, he added a roll. The combination of wet grass and his movement created a tight spiral of cotton that washed all the way to his ankles. He just laid there in confusion as his bare, pasty bottom exposed, and his knotted shorts not so easily restored. Gillen, not one to lose his composure, fixed the problem and returned to his gentle run with an enormous grin on his face. He hoped that this moment would disappear as quickly as the rain had, but a resounding clap assisted him in recognition that everyone played witness to all our tomfoolery.

The thing with distance runners that differs from any other athlete I have met is their comfort in being themselves and not worrying what others think about their actions. Through the years, I have enough stories to make up volumes as plentiful as an encyclopedia collection. There were days, when on gentle runs, where we would run through campus buildings much to the amazement of the students in these buildings. All of us in our short running shorts, often time shirtless, just pacing through the halls as if we did it every day without reservation. On hot days, we plunged into Showalter

Fountain or any waterway in our path. We also had an idea to have theme days every Wednesday on our gentle days. We would wear costumes of some sort that matched the criteria for the day. Jon Teipen, my roommate, a proud graduate of Center Grove High School, secured a mass of uniforms from the early 1970s.

We all arrived in the locker room to pick up our garb. These uniforms were polyester, which did not bode well for a day climbing up into the high 80s. We outfitted ourselves and headed to Billy Hayes Track to stretch per routine. At the beginning of practice, the whole team would run two warm up laps before stretching. Our plan was to run onto the track, fashionably late, as the rest of the team began their laps for impact's sake. We urged each other to keep smiles from our faces and act as if nothing was out of the ordinary. The rest of the team laughed, doubtfully with us, but at us. As the initial surprise wore off, we departed the track and headed out on the infamous campus loop. There was something special about this loop as just hearing its name caused complete relaxation to settle in. Did we attract a lot of attention on our run from the locals? Yes! Was it any different from the catcalls and "run Forest run" comments of the past, not necessarily. No matter how we dressed, costume or not, we were a constant target, especially in the spring months when the fraternity boys littered their porches. Image was not something that concerned us. We were our own niche and the outside world could not stymie our freedom to experience life on our terms.

The simplicity of life was of greatest value. We were not consumed by cell phones, the Internet (still dial up) or video games (minus our Mario Kart battles). Most of the time we lounged in the locker room post run, the training room pre or post workout, training tables (athlete meals held in Memorial Stadium), or just hung out at home. The conversations would often border on the side of ridiculous, never lacking for creativity. Through all the travel together for competitions and living together, there really were no secrets amongst us. There was always someone to hang out with when homework was light, or when you just needed to talk. My teammates became my brothers and my oasis from a life of chaos. We ran into an occasional test of wills, but we loved like family. In one of the most difficult times of life, securing self-identity, I could not have asked for a more solid group of men to provide a clearer understanding of who I was.

Liferide

As my running was coming into focus, my identity became lodged with it. An extreme haze existed when it came to my future. I started as a business major and then shifted into English with an education endorsement. Even though the transition appeared to make sense or at least was a better fit, I was not sure why. There was much I still had to learn about myself and my passions. The first time in my life I followed my cousin Mike proved lucrative, so when my father urged me to reach out again to him regarding a new endeavor, I hesitantly obliged.

It was the summer of my sophomore year of college when I picked up the phone to call my localized hero of a cousin. He asked me to be part of his new creation as a counsellor; there was no chance of saying no. My cousin, Mike Billish, along with his old college teammate, Eddie Slowikowski, were amid developing a non-profit organization by the name of Liferide. The intention was to provide leadership to high school students, empowering them to make the best of themselves through educational opportunities and service. The weeklong camp challenged students to get in touch with their inner selves and help them recognize their unique qualities. Even though the camp was aimed at helping these teenagers, I could have never dreamed it would hold as much for me.

I was caught up living a confused existence trying to find my identity and purpose. The distant question of what my future would look like, amidst a pool of friends who had a clear direction, created an internal struggle to place myself. Two years into my education followed more of a routine "this is what you do" type response. I went to class but was not sure to what end. Even though I had found my fit at Indiana, the clock was ticking on that whole "adult life" program that followed. It was a time of answer seeking that exposed a very sad person confused about life. In my journal, I wrote about this time:

"I have come to the point of ill-satisfaction lately. All my anger and pain lie within one resolve. At this moment, I cannot find inspiration. I have yet to figure out the glory of my supposed self. What else is left? There is too much stress in this world and I often question if I can handle it or not. So, when does my heart get healed? When is it my turn to be happy?"

Just revisiting this dark place gives me chills, but what is readily apparent is when God has a plan, he has a plan. Not only did I build a deeper relationship with my cousin but also my uncle and my cousin's former teammates from Loyola. Liferide gave me the awareness of my unique gifts, but it took time for me to soak it in and move on and live. The first year ultimately served me. It was the therapy I needed to begin the transfer of thoughts from self-loathing to the benefit of others. The hole that I dug was rooted in selfishness. I never reached beyond myself for council; I just gave up... I ran. It was the recognition, that in being myself, I could have a substantial impact on society. When the status quo was more appetizing to my inner being, the nudge to go beyond the limitations I set on myself led to healing. I could have never resurrected from that hole until I realized that I needed to allow someone to pull me out.

Each year I returned for the camps, I felt more complete and could then transfer my strength to others. The basic logic was I could not bleed something that was not present in me; it required restoration before I could be the one to restore. Understanding I was not alone in my struggles was a vital component in providing the ladder for escape. I did not want attention because making this weakness visible to others only made the reality sink further in. Avoidance was my chosen path. The smallest instances would trigger my emotions and it only seemed self-destructive. It scared me; I wanted to run! I felt the way I did when I had problems controlling my anger in elementary school. Those days were full of pain even though self-induced. I felt I was the victim, yet I was the oppressor. It was a time of great suffering for my family and me, and all those feelings smacked me back in the face. I kept thinking about how far I had come and believed that all that progress was now spoiled. I thought there was no way out of my predicament. I was void of the two primary things that brought me life: community and faith.

Ever since I left high school, my drift from the church increased, as finding another environment like what I had was not available. With the pressures I was facing, something had to go, and unfortunately my attendance as well as progression of my faith went with it. I was seeking anything spiritual to replace the euphoric feelings I had once entertained. A major shift took place where I believed in simple acts as a means to a strong faith. I was caring, I did some good things, I prayed, but the depth was limited. There was no organization to the pillars I once stood by.

While absent for an outlet of my faith, this camp came along. This was a leadership camp and not a Bible camp, but it fed me. It provided me an opportunity to work with the youth and share my life. There was no better stamp of approval in my new major choice of education as I truly came to life working with teenagers. An extension of this camp that continued my growth was in the form of mission trips. My spirit found rejuvenation as my life purposes continued to be unveiled. This is what I was built to do; there was no doubt in my mind.

The only reasoning gathered was the saving grace of a loving God. I learned a great deal from my situation and life became that much more of value. As I reread some of my past journal entries, it appalled me. How could I have felt so hopeless? Why did life seem an unconquerable task? It just goes to show how powerful human emotions are. When you let emotions control you, you are against an undefeated opponent. I required a new lens to view life; this camp provided the eye exam. This early movement brought with it some hopeful outlooks. I began to see the positive side of this journey. There was a reason to my suffering, and I required it to shed light on the many gifts surrounding me. This new perspective was exemplified in a writing I penned amidst the experience appropriately titled, *The Ride of Your Life:*

It is in the time in which we actively live, the present, where life is unveiled to us. The destination is not as important as how we get there. A transformation occurs as we grow with one another and we begin to see beyond physical beauty, beyond intellect, beyond social differences and instead into each other's souls. We begin to see what is truly marvelous about others, what they entail as spiritual beings. Our bodies are simply covers that do not always tell the true story about what lies within. It is when we do away with the facade and allow others to share that space of comfort that we can be truly happy and appreciate life for what it is. When the mask is put down, the most dynamic, exhilarating part of us becomes accessible to all we interact with. We become the people we have dreamed to be. Don't ever compromise who you are to fit the molds others try to put you in. Always be true to yourself and that endless stream of beauty will radiate through you. People will be able to see the genuine, unique beauty you possess. The light will find its way into their souls and bring a smile to each face you encounter. You are what you believe. See what you believe and become what you see. Take life one day at a time and bask in every moment. Don't look forward, don't look back, just look! Take the time to see how great you are NOW! If you do this, you are in store for the ride of your life.

Change of Command

College life continued, but after settling into comfort at my second home, things were about to shift once again. As was typical, we would receive mail over the summer from Coach Bell, mostly training regimen or simple check ins. When this letter came in the mail, I fell into shock. In the fall of 1998, Indiana University went through a transformation, or more aptly suited, a metamorphosis. The team was still intact, but our leader was soon to change. Sam Bell coached Indiana through some of the greatest years in collegiate cross country and track & field, but those days were soon to be over. After 29 years, he was hanging it up. His replacement, Dr. Robert Chapman, a young 30 something coach. The litany of titles associated with him that were fed to us included: A member of the United States Olympic Committee and USA Track & Field research on the "Live High - Train Low" altitude training model and the Associate Director of Sport Science and Medicine for USA Track & Field. We were not sold on credentials alone as Bell had his share.

The only thing that would impact us was the practicality of his advisement to our weary team. I sat in disbelief as the reason I chose Indiana was largely in part because of Coach Bell, but now he was gone. Questions of my decision to stay recirculated as I tried to get a handle on the situation. It was like starting over... as a junior. Despite his old school mentality and tough love approach, Coach Bell instilled in me a level of commitment, pride, and tough love. Some of my fondest memories were when him and Fran would host the team at their house. They were like parents who enjoyed the simple pleasure of their children being at home under the same roof. This semblance of a family was an essential comfort. In my estimation, there was no one who could replace him, so whatever body came about would have their work cut out for them. As I tried to hold on to the past and cherish all this man did for me, it reminded me of something that caused me to pause. In his final season, I was awarded the Coaches' Award, which was given to the athlete most disciplined to the purposes of the school and program. To this day, it is still one of the greatest recognitions I have ever received.

Speculation continued to mount as we tried to envision what this new system would look like. A lot of us were sad, but some viewed any change as beneficial to us and a redemption for some of our careers. Most of us had stuck to Coach Bell's training program over the summer as it was our assumed direction, but with the late term shift, most did not know what to expect. We remained hopeful that a single tapping together of the shoes and we would move back to the top of the NCAA in relevancy. It was a naïve and fantastical thought, but that is the gift of new seasons.

Chapman's arrival was at an interesting time. Most of his runners were juniors or seniors who had run a very different program in the past. To transfer that mental/emotional direction on such notice would appear an impossible task, yet Chapman tried. Other changes included the flight of Marius, which was an additional bump as now two of my mentors instantly vanished. The early stages of the Chapman era were rough. He had basically no knowledge of us outside of a stat sheet and was trying to determine ways to make us tick. What often happens in times of change, there was resistance. I am not sure where the high and mighty viewpoint came from considering we were bottom feeders in the Big Ten the year previous.

As the program fell into transition, the meaning behind the uniform was dimly lit. An Indiana jersey was now just a preface to a story about another program fallen by the wayside. As the years passed with a transition marked through coaching change, the staleness of our pride was more obvious than ever before. We had lost faith in our running, our team, and ourselves. I remember the first day we met Coach Chapman was during physicals in the training room. As we all sat there waiting for our turn to see the doctor, I was targeted as Chapman noticed the Auburn cross country shirt I was wearing. There was no personal attachment to the school, just something I had picked up during my sisters' college competitions. I was ashamed that I did not recognize what this symbolic event meant. This infuriated our new coach; what a tremendous welcome showing where our minds were. We had settled into running as recreation.

With time, Chapman resorted to his strength, science. He tested us in ways I was not familiar with. This new form of training put us often in a lab. He may not have known what motivated us, but he knew how we could be transformed. He was meticulous in his studies, and despite a learning curve and an egg drop of a cross country season, we saw progress. Chapman had an uncanny way of delivering confidence. He stated times our bodies told him we could run. It was hard not to believe it. The cross country season was used as an experiment as all scientists do. This sacrifice of a season was difficult on all of us. We were seeing progression in workouts, but it was not translating to meets.

Chapman tried every trick in the book, and it was difficult for us to see the grand scheme as we finished a dismal tenth place at the Big Ten Championships. There was no question of the variance from Bell. His form of motivation was more logic based than bold challenge. It was through recipes in training that would allow us to reach our full potential. He told a group of us we would win the Big Ten crown in the distance medley relay. All of us were skeptical at first, but the thought lingered and further ingrained itself in us. Every day was one day closer to that goal. We were ready to win. We figured we had nothing to lose, no one would see it coming. This mentality is what the entire team adopted and our pitiful cries of "woe is me" silenced. It was time to rise from the ashes. Making the connection from the old to the new was not something Chapman could accomplish alone. There was one person who knew how to ignite the fire that had laid dormant for some time, Matt Sparks. With his eligibility complete, he became the sounding board for Chapman's plans, but he had one secret weapon, he knew us. Sparks found his fit and purpose during this time. One of the most difficult things to do is to coach those you competed with. This was not the case with Matt. From the time of our arrival, there was a great respect for him, and he had already accomplished what I speak to many of my athletes, he earned his voice. Sparks had a subtle intensity and a way of relating to us. He became the bridge allowing for a successful transition of coaches.

Old habits are hard to break, but with the transition of coaches, my focus left my former habit of running for others. It took a major change in my life and the understanding that my time in this position was not forever. I never wanted to end my career saying that running was a burden. The face of reality stared me down which brought about the realization that few people had the opportunities I had. I was given a talent, and if I did not embrace it, it would discard the blessing. As a man now in his 40s, I know that the fountain of youth continually dries up, at least from a physical standpoint. Chapman delivered the antidote for my yearning for praise. He successfully shifted my attention off others and onto what he learned my body could achieve. I began to consume my thoughts in training with first, that I was fortunate to be in the position I was in, and second, adjust my energies from external to internal. My relationship with the clock and my heart cleared the path.

Coming to Terms

Maybe I became so caught up in what others thought because I never really accomplished anything in my early years. Possibly, I defaulted to athletics for validation instead of discovering the great many other attributes given to me. Either way, this new consciousness delivered much more to me that elevated beyond athletics. I lived an existence where I felt there was an expectation I had to live up to and doing what others supposed me to do was minus reward. Going back to my youth, the behaviors I entertained became the wrinkles I will spend the rest of my life overcoming. Many people's failures result from what they believe others may think of their choices or performances. The crowd has a strong presence in not only my life, but I am sure many of yours. The revelation came late in my career, but it returned me to the days where running was pure joy. I battled myself for too long and it granted me no particular benefit outside of loss. It was time to see this gift in a new way and not as a burden. I needed to take advantage of this time as what remained was momentary.

Sometimes we question if we are on the right path. Even if we are following the path that leads to all our dreams, it is a guarantee that there will be bumps and potholes. There is not a perfect path to follow. If we live for seamless perfection, we will become void of what is important, and the struggles will be many. I was continually trapped amidst dream chasing when a halt in activity took place whether an injury, poor performance or general funk. I would wonder if there was something different out there and then immediately redirect my mission. I wanted to be the best runner I could be. I wanted this, I wanted that, but I was limited in staying power. I would decide too quickly once complications arose and bury that present dream for a new possibility. This led me to squander opportunities only to question myself in the next endeavor.

This was a continuous cycle in my early life because I avoided failure. Funny thing to reflect and realize I failed more so resultant of the avoidance. Friendships became distant because of a trying time, jobs resigned because of a conflict, and opportunities replaced with conflicting opportunities. The simple truth is the past is the past. We can try to duplicate what something was, but it will never be the same. We must live with mistakes; we must live with failure, but it need not hold us captive. We need to reconcile the past so we can have a future. All of us make mistakes; it does not matter the degree. I have watched this play itself out too many times in my life and enough was enough.

Every person's progression chart looks different. Some learn through difficulties early and others much later. The important thing here is that we learn. The team I coach now is not one team I ran for or one team I have coached previously. There is a unique quality to each that may be marred by comparison if we do not continually reinvent ourselves and our perspective. The results won't be the same, conversely, probably worse off because we keep jamming the circle peg in the square. Matthew Broderick in his role as Ferris Bueller states it best, "Life moves pretty fast. If you don't stop and look around once in a while, you could miss it." I am guilty of this even today, but I was done taking things for granted and living to please others. Life was passing me by, and I was missing out on all the snapshot moments. It had to be about more, not just the training or the race, but all the truly meaningful things that came with it: family, friends, experience, and growth. The time was now; it was the only option.

To Run

Time to Rise

Indiana was mostly ineffectual in the Big Ten conference from a distance perspective. With cross country in the rear-view mirror, we realigned ourselves for the indoor campaign. For the first time in three years, we were not only fit, but a wave of health encompassed the team. Performances popped early and our depth was becoming more and more clear. We were being fed by solid racing, but for me, one dent interfered. Two weeks out from the Indoor Big Ten Championships I began to have an issue with my knee (tendinitis) that was not being healed with conventional methods. They moved me to the pool, and I entertained some of Jim Spivey's aqua training from his time at IU. The workouts were intense; it was an odd sensation to sweat in a pool, but discomfort was of no consequence since time was of the essence.

With our redemption meet only weeks away, my knee was improving, so we applied a test. They entered me in the 800 meters at the Hoosier Hills Invitational. It was a meet that had preliminaries and finals. Ideally, I would get a rust buster and then an opportunity to see where I was at. The preliminary was not spectacular, but what needed to be done was done; I qualified for finals as the number two seed to one of my teammates. In addition, my legs suffered no damage. Overall, I felt relatively strong. In the final I began to sense that the pool training did its job, and I was still fit. I continued to move through the field coming into the final straightaway when a burst of energy sprung through me and propelled me into the lead taking the title. Winning did not hurt my hopes of making Big Tens memorable as all other doubts faded.

The week arrived and our departure for the University of Wisconsin began what we believed to be a defining moment for the distance contingent. On day one of the contest, there is only one final event, the distance medley relay, which they slated me to run the 800-meter leg. Leading up to the race, we were absent from the track facility altogether using the indoor football practice center. As we were doing our final stretches, Coach Chapman asked if I was ready to go. I responded boldly, "I am ready to win!" I am not sure where this came from, but it told the story of the transformed athletes we now were.

Much of my thought leading up to this race was not fear driven, but more opportunity driven. I wanted to race; I was ready. The gun interrupted my thoughts as my eyes set on Mikko, our 1200 leg. After the 600-meter mark, he had shifted to the front half of the pack and exchanged in third place. Our 400 leg then took over and held our position. Trent was nearly impossible to pass because of his size and dwarfed the remaining members of our relay. The time had come, and I was standing in third position awaiting his arrival. With a late charge and a seamless handoff, I sat in second behind Purdue. My leg was uneventful early on, as I sat on the shoulder of the leader but knew the time had come. As I hit the final backstretch, I was blasted as if from a canon. Over the last 150 meters, I had opened a 30-meter lead. The final leg was here, and Aaron stretched things out more.

As is typically the case in the DMR, the final leg was a who's who of Big Ten talent. By no means did we believe the race was in the bag as a pack of four surged and surpassed Aaron 600 meters in. They were working for sure, but Aaron hung in there. It was looking like the race would end in a mad dash with the ordering of finishers as predictable as pulling names from a hat. I did not have a sense how fast these guys were going, but as Aaron put in a long winded 500-meter kick, the rest fell out of contention and this unlikely crew became Big Ten Champions. Later, in reviewing splits, Aaron went out in 57 seconds for his first quarter which means the field that dragged him back were clear mid to low 50s, a good reason they could not respond when Aaron decided to go. We were the first

Hoosiers to win a DMR Big Ten title in the school's history; the second group was not added until 2017.

This was a forever moment and what happened after that became history. Compiling all the struggles we faced as a team and individually, to have the validation for the work we put in was beyond gratifying. Performance after performance during those championships marked a new era for Indiana. The ripples it sent though the Big Ten were only eclipsed by the engagement of new recruits. People now started to see something more tangible. What this movement would become was the next layer of Chapman's plans. He had won us over, but we were upperclassman heavy. The question of program sustentation had to be addressed.

We then saddled the mental rebranding of team expectations with a proposal to recruit the top athletes in Indiana. Chapman was not alone in this belief, the token fifth year seniors believed it as well. We began to see it as our legacy. Indiana being a mediocre program was not what we came here for. Our willingness to sacrifice for the vision of Coach Chapman provided the spark to accompany the fuel.

Mentally, we were all trying to stay afloat as our time at Indiana was running out. This ingenious plot, The Team Indiana Project, was aimed at recruiting the best athletes the state offered; however, this idea was not the genius, as many before had gone backyard shopping. A twist at this time, Indiana was not a top tier program, so the sell was a greater challenge. Chapman did not have much of a history in the state, but in his time at IU in his first stint, he knew that there was plenty of talent to serve his purposes. What he ended up comprising was a packet that hypothesized what the past would have looked like had the Indiana high school products joined forces at IU and what it could look like with our new prospective athletes. The simple answer, a slew of top five NCAA finishes. This all in approach may have been lofty to many, but not us.

We became salesmen in every sense of the word. Everything we did was now amplified and our performances were the fodder to crack the door of interest. In its most basic form, we were selling ourselves which was a necessary component. When we brought in this stellar class on a recruitment weekend, the hope was that we would feed no false information or elevate ourselves, but lift these boys, the future. Having had worked in sales at a stage in my life I know one thing: if you have success, you are a great liar, or you truly believe in your product. These guys saw something in us that made them want to join us in this endeavor minus smoke and mirrors. We forever are known as "the seniors" to this group and we, together, started a resurgence. The rally cry we shared which matched our team personality and coach was that "we're feeling much better now". We finally broke the oppressive chains of our past, and there was no looking back.

Brief Glimpse

When I was in high school, I made a promise to myself. When you are a runner, you deal with the physical deformity of being skinny. I used to lift weights often, but no additional weight gain occurred. It was an enjoyable past time, maybe just because it offered a break from the redundancy of crushing mile upon mile on the roads. When I became serious in running, a lot of the sports I used to enjoy were eliminated because they had the potential of injury or from being too tired to operate once the daily mileage had been put in. I was not obsessed with "getting big", but it is a common thread in the high school realm. Just like trying to grow a beard upon the first morsel of facial hair, there was a natural curiosity. I vowed to check this off my "to do" list as soon as my running career ended.

This period of life still seemed quite a distance off; however, a freak occurrence my junior year provided a head start into the bulk phase of life resultant of an illness that was not clearly defined. It held me in my room for over a week, sidelined from school and practice. I sweat through every article of clothing I wore putting a damper on sleep as I was suffering from a severe case of the chills. Nobody knew what was wrong with me and I refused a doctor visit early on because just moving threw off my equilibrium. Daylight offered an additional reason to hide away; it was like a searing, scarring light. I did not eat for days, but never had the want for food anyhow. I was afraid, as anyone would be, to tempt my stomach with its distaste for all. After seeing a doctor and being put on heavy antibiotics, I began to emerge from the grave. I was 119 pounds, 24 less than my standard weight when all was said and done. This did not change my decision to try and savor my outdoor track season. My coach fished some ideas, and the decision was to put me on creatine to see if I could pick up some mass and regain strength. This plan undoubtedly failed as training at a meaningful level in my feeble state did not seem to work.

To "give it a go," I jumped in a race at Purdue University. My recollection of that race was minimal, amounting to only the first 200 meters. From others' descriptions, I swayed in the final 100 meters covering lanes 1-8, back and forth, eventually collapsing at the line in a masterful 2:12. I never ran an 800 meters that slow going all the way back to grammar school. It was a telltale sign that the season had to be bagged. This experience left me distraught as I returned to campus with my season in the wastebasket. Minus running for the time being, I hit the weight room, as it was always a confidence booster in the past. There was one small difference, one

I did not note in the early going; I was still taking the rest of the creatine. Before I knew it, I ballooned to 160 pounds and could hardly manage a gentle five miles. Once I bounced back to health, and the creatine ran out, my journey back down to my racing weight commenced. The time lost through this ordeal left me with little option outside of red shirting my senior cross country season to reestablish a base. I got a taste of what it was like to be "bigger," but I still had running goals to accomplish. My herculean gain expired, but I was certain I would renew my membership at some point.

In my return to functional human form, the greatest difficulty was running exclusively to bring my weight down. The additional force added from my elevated size was not doing me any favors as it quickly triggered issues from my back down. The bike became my go between. With some money I had saved, I made the largest investment in my life at that point, a new Trek road bike. This was a big deal considering the bike I had throughout college was an $89 Iron Horse. I'm not even sure if that was the brand, although it did the job in getting me to classes and practice. Back to my investment, a cold $1000. I second guessed this decision many times, but it turned out to be worth it and the bike still exists in the Billish quarters today. The weight began to drop as my old form returned even though a comeback to running was difficult. This life interruption was viewed as a prerequisite to restoration. It became abundantly clear that at the core, I was a runner; this break was a gentle reminder. The hunger to run after this hiatus was natural, but as I sit here a four-time Ironman finisher, getting my bearings on the bike was not all bad.

One Final Push

The Team Indiana project was no longer in its formative days and the addition of a stellar freshmen class was the result. It was time to get to work. Nothing was automatic, but the added bodies upped the competition level of all. The blending of personalities was of little consequence as, despite our seniority, this group of youngsters had a flare, something that had been missing. Their talent extended beyond running, and the famous Room 207 was born. The musical talents of a handful of guys spurned this band along, unfortunately, with a handful of front man turnover. They honored me with the role for a brief time fulfilling my bucket list item of singing in a band. The band was just the start of the new wave. It was odd as the elders; we provided a familiarity of protocol and an energy fueled by our desperation to advance, but they had their own personality. They were the social epicenter of the team led by Chris Powers. Chris could be the most intense person when in relation to competition, but outside he had a circle of influence and natural leadership. It looked as if we knew where the baton would be passed. Maybe we were as goofy in our earlier years, but I think all the conflict we had faced through time absorbed our swagger. We were like parents who struggled to stay in the loop; all of us had some desire to be the "cool" parent. My intention here is not to say that we were castaways, but the introduction of the new breed with years of success ahead of them, and us, on our way out, created a varied perspective.

In one year, we climbed out from the cellar of the Big Ten finishing fifth at the championships and ninth in the Great Lakes Region with limited freshmen activated. The previous year, we did not even field a complete team at regionals. The focal year was now upon us. Having had red shirted my senior year to reestablish strength after my illness, this was my last shot. We were now fifth year seniors with a core of sophomores. Even though there was great excitement with the added horsepower, every workout, every race was business like. We dominated the Indiana Intercollegiate after someone disturbed our streak the year before. The team champion plaque is not housed in any place of tribute as we burned it. We were hungry and intense. Relishing in any performance was viewed as futile since our plans were much greater. The decision was to dismiss the luxury busses and instead opt for passenger vans. This move continued the trend of limiting any kind of distraction as we used to travel with the women's program. Outright, we returned to necessities as we believed whatever would be given to us had to be earned.

Nothing mattered accomplishment wise early on as the only thing that would mark our return to the national stage would be us literally lining up at the NCAA Championships. Before that could become a reality, we needed to take on our conference which brought us to The University of Wisconsin, a place I had fond memories from my high school days as a camper and from winning a Big Ten title in track my junior year. This had to be the place where my next memory would be made... it was fate.

We had to be the most lopsided underdogs going into the meet with outside expectation nonexistent. The difference was, we did not view ourselves that way. We had a belief we were elite and anything minus a top three finish would be a dismal affair. The race was a blur, but when the final tally came, they revealed Indiana as the Big Ten runner up to future national runner-up, Wisconsin. To say that we were not pleased with the performance would be false, but nothing came from this event outside of increasing confidence; it did not secure us a bid to the national championships. Our public guise remained constant, but the drive home was a different story. Chapman led the disc jockey efforts, which he had done occasionally during workouts blasting his vintage rock, as we joined in the singing of Queen's "We Are the Champions" despite not winning the meet. We were overcoming our demons and recent past. We celebrated the moment with the only people aware of the sacrifices made to be in that position. The approval beyond ourselves was unnecessary. No parade, outside acknowledgment or pats on the back, just looking into the eyes of my brothers knowing we were not done yet.

Regionals was on tap, and this would be the determining factor if we would make the trip to Ames, Iowa for the NCAA Championships. It is basically the Big Ten meet all over again with additional talent including Notre Dame and Eastern Michigan. These just happened to be the two teams that edged us out along with meet champion, Wisconsin. With All-Region performances by Aaron Gillen and Chad Andrews, we were hopeful. College results are interesting in terms of the qualifying stages for cross country. The top two teams earn automatic bids, whereas the rest idly sit by and wait for the at large process to take place. This included an evaluation of team compiled stat sheets throughout the season somewhat like March Madness. What big wins over qualifying teams were had and were there any clunk performances? They hosted the race in Ypsilanti, Michigan, home of Eastern Michigan University, on Saturday, but our future was not to be determined until the following Monday. When the call came, since the Internet was not quite at full efficiency in disseminating information, there was more a sigh than a celebration. The reinforcement of our goal and our commitment to it supplied the calm. The day would come when we could look back on this season and enjoy it, but today wasn't it.

As the attention shifted to the final staple of the season, the only out of ordinary action included the uniforms. The past uniforms we had adorned over our years were nondescript, difficult to identify who we were. Now was the time for us to strip away the rags. We made the final decision to wear the uniform Bob Kennedy did in his senior campaign. It was a positive vibe thread, but the University did not stockpile these past outfits. At the conclusion of each year, the Geiger House, otherwise known as the cross country and track & field house, put on a quarter sale. Any gear from past seasons was available to purchase. It was like Christmas day for a runner as we could show up with ten dollars and leave with forty pieces of gear. Since the vintage jersey I wore as a freshman was in the pile, I loaded up, roughly eight singlets. These were the desired jersey the team wanted to wear at nationals. I was more than accommodating to "loan" my jerseys out which, to this day, are still on loan. The jerseys represented so much more to us after this season and I cannot blame any of them for their failure to return it.

One more meet on the schedule as we were off to Ames, Iowa, and Iowa State University. From my history, I can fairly say that my involvement in anything cross country post season was jinxed. I always ran my high school state cross country meets under miserable conditions and it seems ever since I transitioned into coaching, the weather magically has been beyond ideal. Unfortunately, as an athlete, this trend continued, and Ames was brutally cold. The course lived amongst fields, so there was absolutely no block from the elements. The basic strategy was simple, stay warm, which was an impossible task on that day. The course was a ghost town prior to the start, as most camps were on busses or in the lobby of the dormitories. Many teams even put in their warmup miles indoors running in place or down small corridors. No one was looking forward to the call to the starting line knowing what they were about to walk into. One last-minute change was the addition of Kevin Chandler to the top seven, just ten minutes before being called to the line. Without intention on running that day, he logged eight miles that morning and resolved his hunger with a big McDonald's breakfast.

Kevin, despite being a year behind us, was an honorary fifth-year senior because of his hard working nature and unmatched maturity. He was also the only teammate I had known prior to my arrival in Bloomington. We both attended the Wisconsin Camp of Champions and were in the same training group we labeled the "Foot Long Gumby's" my senior year of high school. Because of this statistic, Coach Bell decided it best I accompany him to a dinner with Kevin and his family on his recruiting visit. If there was ever a time someone applied hot coals to me, it was during this casual meal when Kevin's father blatantly addressed the injury bug surrounding the team. Cool and collected, I went to bat for my coach and the rest is history. Either way, this switch up matched the chaos of the day. I think none one of us would have thought the championships would be so dismal. I had imagined soaking in every ounce of that day, but the number one priority was returning to the heated dormitories post-race. It could not have been more opposite from our visit here for pre-nationals when it was absurdly warm and humid. The race came and went without many stellar performances. The winning time was one of the slowest winning times in history, not for lack of talent, but the human body was not cut out for such an environment. Gillen ran phenomenally well, just on the bridge of All-American status. Under the classification of All-American today, he would have been. Our youth and inexperience at this level also played into the result, but we managed a 17th place finish and the season and our intensity found relief. We could finally celebrate the gallant return of Indiana distance running and we passed the figurative baton to the "freshmen."

To Run

The Beginnings End

At the conclusion of my fifth year of eligibility in cross country, I had one more season available to use, outdoor track. An added note, my academic career completed in December. How perfect, right? Spend the entire indoor season with no other distractions and ramp up for my final season. That view changed with our Big Ten runner up performance and NCAA top 20 finish in cross country. After the labor of debated transfer, coaching change and the intensity of training, I was fatigued, and my vision was not clear. In retrospect, I view the decision as idiotic, but my mental state won out.

As soon as cross country was over, I joined my roommates/teammates aptly tagged as "The Nates" on a run. It was a cold winter day with a light snow on the ground that covered the grass, leaving the streets clear, but slick. We were running a seven miler in Blue Ridge, a Sam Bell staple, and we had reached about the five-mile mark when my legs just stopped moving. It was the oddest thing considering I was hardly winded; they just gave up on me. It was as if my legs were telling me something. Before my company could ask what was up, I said, "I'm done!" They looked at me as if I were nuts as I repeated the phrase. They continued their run, thinking maybe I was just hanging it up for the day, but it was more definitive to me. I believed my time as a competitive runner was over and I was ready to move on. I always wondered what that final decision would look when I stepped away. It made little sense to me, but perfect sense all the same. When I was left alone walking, the simple pleasure of the trees and snow took me; it was breathtaking. I had run this course probably over one hundred times and never noticed its beauty. It was a reawakening telling me it was time to slow down, avert my focus, and enjoy the simplicity of life. For the first time I had made a decision I did not question. It just felt right.

In the absence of running, my need for some activity to fill the space opened the door to returning to the weight room. I quickly found myself in a regimented strength program courtesy of the IU weight room staff. The opportunity I had was unmatched. I was at a Big Ten school with full access to the training facilities and professionals to help guide me. I became an everyday weight room guest; some days I would even be in there twice a day. The newness of this endeavor created much excitement as I began to treat it like running. I had goals and my training was intense. I did not notice how much bigger I was becoming, although my teammates did. I was not Arnold Schwarzenegger, but to a distance guy, same thing. In a short time, I had graduated to 180 pounds. My dream of being big came true, but it came with some baggage. When I was average or below average weight wise, I was calm, a natural sweetheart. When people knocked me around, I was quick to even apologize myself and walk away. Not anymore, I knew now I could back myself; the prototypical "tough guy" mentality was attached. I found myself entangled in a lot more drama than before which began to change who I was. It was with this realization that led to my early retirement in the lifting department and the battle back to mid-grade fitness began. Besides my new size, I realized that a lot of things I used to enjoy were things I could hardly do anymore. What is the point of getting so strong that the only thing you could do is be strong? These repetitive "breaks" reminded me of my early days of running avoidance. This stalking friend refused to let me free. Running was like a boomerang; it always returned no matter how hard I threw it. Maybe I wasn't supposed to let it go.

To Run

Home is Where...

I now had lived the muscle man lifestyle, and despite my thought of some form of glamour, I wasn't cut out for it. The running bug bit again as it had so many times. I returned to live with my parents upon graduation; however, there was an address change from my childhood home. The coziness and comfort were not necessarily there as I had just lived with close friends for the past four years. Either way, it was time to become an adult and find a job. I landed a job rather quickly as a high school English teacher. That summer I became an assistant coach for the cross country and track & field teams. I decided that I would train, but just enough to run with the high school guys I was working with. This sounded a lot easier said than done as erasing my competitive flare and training standard ended up a daunting task. I became obsessive resorting to all that I knew, which was my college mentality and workload. I was hired in March for a job that did not start until August. What else was I supposed to do? Training seemed to be the most logical option. I also took my first crack at program design and sorted through what I had picked up over the years. After countless hours of coaching and running with my team, I continued to watch others reach for

145

their dreams. It was running with these guys I began to realize where I belonged. I loved coaching but could not move on from my running, which was conflicting. I was not ready to let go of this season and that did not allow me to move on to embrace the next challenge. I was not ready for adulthood; I still wanted to play. As my fitness progressed, the question arose, to what end? If I would run, I would train for something. No marathons or road races, I wanted to go back to the track. It rekindled the fire, and it marked yet another return.

I was amidst the track season when things began to go awry at my job. It shattered my innocence as my switch to education was to leave the "winner takes all" mentality of the business world. Maybe it was professional immaturity or an unwillingness to acquiesce to a systematic plot. In the general scope, I knew I would return to education, but I felt too young to have a substantial impact on students merely four years younger than me. I needed space and time. I am a firm believer that all things happen for a reason. This very difficult time of life provided me with a window to chase my dream of competing at the Olympic Trials. Ever since I was in high school, my dad and coach told me I was a miler, but since I had attained much success in the 800, I never really gave it an honest shot. I finished college as a legitimate 800-meter runner, but I had reached a limit in that event. My speed would not take me to that next level. For this to happen, I needed a community of support.

When all else fails, move to Bloomington? I returned to Indiana University to live and train under my college coach, Dr. Robert Chapman. After I sat out a year wondering if this was truly the end of my running career, I had an awakening or modern inconvenience, depending on how you see it. In my final years under Chapman, I finally started to figure things out and believed there was much left untapped to explore. First things first, I needed to check the pulse of my coach. I was nervous because I questioned if he even believed it was a good idea or based on all the constructive criticism from those around me, if I even believed. Questions of my talent and potential came under scrutiny; I believed others saw my dream as unattainable. Coach Chapman related my current situation to a questionable time in his own life that relieved my insecurities. He was more than supportive and secured me a job as a University Athletic Tutor to work under a less stressful environment while making enough money to get by. My old college roommate, Tom Chorny, also had his eyes set on Bloomington as he continued his professional career. Many former teammates remained, which is logical considering I was only a year removed.

Under the direction of Chapman, IU appeared to be climbing the ranks of respectability. Chorny was crowned the 2001 United States National Steeplechase champion with goals of someday owning the American record. With the addition of Footlocker finalists, Sean and

John Jefferson and Stephen Haas, the appeal of the community only grew. Despite the initial plan of moving to Bloomington to establish a base before joining some old teammates in route to California, I stalled, feeling like this might just be the best environment for me, potentially the end route.

California was instilled in me during January 2002. I thought I needed a weather change to serve my running interests best. With my buddy Aaron in Santa Barbara, it seemed to be the best environment to focus solely on my goal. I needed an escape from my current situation which required moving somewhere. The more I settled at IU, the further this move got pushed back. The options in Bloomington appeared limitless. There was no place on the planet where I would have rather been. I blame this thought on simple familiarity and comfort. My early training was mostly building my strength base, so I hopped in here and there with the team on their lighter days. The most bizarre recognition was that this was a different team. Despite many of my former teammates being present, the dynamic had shifted; the "freshmen" were now guiding the ship. I tried to allow the space for this team to be what they were without me superimposing past standards on them. I just felt old and out of place. It was still home, but some paint started to crack.

To Run

My unwelcome visitor returned in the form of depression. The interesting thing is that I always believed with will power and time, this foe could ultimately be defeated. The problem was that this was the third visit in a reasonably short amount of time. Based on experience, my descent to rock bottom was all too common. I had floated in and out of waves feeling that life was no longer valuable, that my purpose absolved, and the world would benefit from my exit. I continually question who or what had gotten a hold of me at these times. I moved back to Bloomington full of hope; it offered an escape. Very simply, I ran. This response mechanism was common every time a new environment challenged me. It made sense with my limited outlet in terms of my faith, that I harnessed all burdens unto myself which always led to some collapse. With this life of escapism, the questions lingered why I felt the need to run or what I was running to.

To Run

Running Alone

As a runner, sometimes you need to be alone. Times when the only way for you to return to competition is to run on your own and reevaluate your situation while refocusing your goals. I have been in this position many times throughout my career. The most recent decent into seclusion was not the therapeutic kind. This was not a time for a checkup, rather, a check out. My time alone was not only limited to runs. This depression cycle had no definitive expiration date. It is a sad time because running is normally the answer to all my problems, but when it becomes part of the problem, I am unable to escape my rough days. During a good run or even a poor run, I can feel a charge of energy. This energy is then sapped, and I feel there is no one to turn to except myself. The ingrained masculinity is hampering disallowing aide during a time like this because it reveals weakness. If you can overcome your own obstacles, then you get stronger, right? This small voice continues its onslaught of suggestion. Depending on your mind's direction, it could be inspired encouragement or contribute to a complete shutdown of life. When vulnerability is present, it becomes an even more convincing, manipulative voice. Each time I thought had overcome this thorn, it made an unexpected return and more painful than its predecessor. Motivation is lacking when that resounding noise tells you to take a day off to recover. It is entrancing in its spell and it is easier to accept the misaligned wisdom, but it is not the answer. When this thought crossed my mind, the workout was doomed, and probably subsequent workouts. Each day the struggle to move forward falls away, but the voice does not leave, it returns the next morning, echoing the same sentiment. Simple suggestions do not appear detrimental, but the culmination of whispers quickly reconstruct the way life is viewed disabling progression.

I forcefully pulled myself out of the rut time and time again, but where was I to go from here? I left college to become an adult, gave up on it, transferred to dream chasing with a location change and made my way somewhere else. I survived that instance, but the issue still loomed. Teleporting was the simplest answer. Leave the problem behind, but I was always brining it with since I did not understand what the real problem was. I had everything a runner could ask for at my disposal, but I could not use it. All excuses come into play on these days or even weeks. The biggest fallacy is what is interpreted as alone is actually lonely. The solution in these moments is not exclusion but inclusion. We need to be around people otherwise the demon continues to have its way. Running alone is often rejuvenating and a prerequisite for healthy thought and contemplation. Running lonely is damaging as the vicious cycle is only prolonged if not worsened as negative thought upon negative thought creep from the subconscious into the conscious. Sometimes you have no choice and the only way to get by is through it.

To Run

Insight and Prophecy

My want and a supposed need were to be alone, but that was not God's plan. I always believed there was some organic sequencing in life, but it more so appeared not as something concrete, mainly abstract. A lot had happened, and most would not consider it a blessing, but I never saw it as a burden, rather, an opening door, a place to run out of. I mentioned earlier my sour ending at my first teaching job, but it created an opportunity for exploration. I was very much lost and followed the nudge to leave that situation. I thought with running, and the comfort of a place that defined me would push me forward. Running became the excuse for my departure. It was the most logical response I had to a time of uncertainty. I did not know if it was the answer, yet my peace was delivered in a simple task, to run. If this is truly what I was called to, I had plenty of time to figure it out. The prospect of what this time could become gave my spirit some light. I was tutoring, running, and writing. I went from a great job to being unemployed to being wealthy again. This wealth was not monetary; I felt fed in a new way. It expanded my vision as I saw the plethora of opportunities in front of me. When one door closed, three doors opened. I always had a knack for quick detachment which had its benefits, although the storage locker of ignorance continued to overfill. These were the times that my life decisions would come to a head. You can't run from everything even though my life mantra to this point was not the antithesis but the rule. Transform your will, transform your life. We often will sit and wait for someone to deliver good fortune to our doorstep. We can wait for a very long time.

The first of these insights was established early upon my return to Bloomington as the general malaise was deafening. Although I had suffered from depression to a degree in college, this was my first real dance with the terror. I intentionally separated myself from human contact. Socially, this might have been a problem, but it put a damper on my running. Excuses were easy to find, and I started to limit my runs not in complete solace so that no new conflicts could be introduced or to erase offers to help. I was looking to do with my time what I wanted to do, which created a massive pile of wasted space. I did not sit at my computer and drill out pages for my book, hang out with friends, or log any meaningful miles. Productivity looked very much like someone playing video games, ordering in every day and watching television. I was slowly falling away from my dreams and newfound life. As was much the trend early in my life, all that bright eyed perspective eventually would wear off. These once glamorized talking points about my next step turned into idle chatter. I had aspirations; I had no desire.

It was even difficult for me to leave my apartment where I lived alone. In this complex there was a nice pool, that for over a month I had never visited. The verbal assault in my head raged as I contemplated a shakeup in my routine. I walked out the door yet stood on my porch not fully convinced of my decision. As I stumbled forward and away from my comfort, I started a symbolic search for identity. The quick exit was necessary before I had the chance to trap myself again and so I quickly grabbed a distraction tool to accompany me to the pool. This random pulling of literature resulted in "The Celestine Prophecy" which I didn't even know existed on my shelves. When I arrived at the pool, I absorbed the sun and the early pages. Sheer enjoyment was not the key, but distraction, as I'm not one to "lay out." I needed some activity.

Sentence after sentence piled up and then I noticed an intruder bringing the number of attendees to two. We exchanged greetings, and I went back to the book although I had to pause after reflecting on her answer. It was not the casual "hello" or "how are you" which boringly spilled from my mouth. Not only did she say, "I am excellent," it was the vibrancy accompanying it. My self-esteem and energy were as close to gutter like as they could be. Her response was a back head slap; it jarred me. I attempted to dive back into the book when an uncanny feeling came upon me, like I was being watched. My self-loathing viewpoint interpreted the actions occurring as something fantastical, but gruesome. A figure continued to descend on me. I wished it was a muskrat who had crept his way into the pool and was about to make havoc of my initial visit rather than another human. My imagination was incorrect, and it was the girl. Nothing extraordinary took place during this conversation, but it was the dialogue I was missing while sitting on my couch at home. My limited option in remaining solo was to let the voice rule. The introduction of another supplied the mute button for that voice. The pool was the first step in acknowledging that life is not to be lived by yourself. My derailment was seeing improvement, one positive interaction at a time.

The simple decision of going to the pool opened the door again and this time it was an escape saving me from myself. This act alone is not what caused my eyes to open wider; it presented more of a panoramic view of the life I was living. What is it in life that cuts off our vision? I was seeing the world through squinted eyes and all my thoughts were manipulated. For it was only what I thought I saw as far as living fully when my eyes were pierced shut again and again by myself. It is a sad thing when we do not see all that the world offers us because of limiting ourselves. This lacking perspective creates routine. When a person falls into a routine, they become stale. They fall into an endless cycle of repetition and nothing of value comes from it. Something caught me in this cycle. Before it became a permanent impairment, a person was delivered that gave pause to the negative self-talk. I ran from one thing to another, but this pattern required disruption.

I would be lying if I said I was financially secure in my early post collegiate days, and I wish I could say that I found the simple joys in each day and moment. Today there are few days I even think about money. Once the transaction with the debtor is finalized, I do not worry about how much money I have or do not have. At this stage though, I could not escape the reality. As a college graduate, the one thing I sought was independence. When money came to the forefront and threatened to compromise my hopes for the future, I couldn't help but question my initial move. It was not entirely well thought out, and the debate rattled on as to what would satisfy me and where could happiness be found. I have watched far too many people fall into the trap transforming into machines for societal acceptance, but they squandered their lives. This was not appealing, but things were not entirely hunky-dory where I stood either. How can someone chase dreams without the means to do so? I was mostly responsible for my plight through irresponsible decisions that pulled money from my pocket, but it was in those provincial moments it became clearer what was of value to me. There is no greater soul searching that could take place then when you are broke. I strongly advise it! A complete healing did not come in this moment, but an acknowledgement is all it took. The most basic thing I did was open myself to others. No matter your position in life, community is key. My reflection on my past challenged me to evaluate the circumstances where I felt pure joy and where growth could be documented. Nothing that made this list was an independent venture. My senior year of high school I was the recipient of the "Rice Pride" award. It may appear trivial and nonsensical, something that would not make the resume of life, but my recollection of my high school years is fond. The most important take away is that I was part of something bigger than myself. At this stage I found purpose and satisfaction. Humans were not designed to be self-sufficient; we were built for interaction! I was not meant to do this alone!

California Dreaming

The assumption I freed myself of whatever burdens I was carrying was not the case. I went to a place of freedom that provided me with so much throughout my college years, and I had support from the community, yet it was not enough. The lockdown was halted a weekend when some former teammates came down, specifically Tom Brooks. He noted my condition immediately; in a short time, after a few runs, we concluded that I needed to stockpile my money, move into a healthier environment, and prepare for the next step. That next step came about rather quickly; the California Dream was reignited. It was early fall when this decision was made with California sitting on a January departure date. I wouldn't say my depression completely subsided, but the distraction was enough for me to divert my attention to something else.

When I moved back to Palos Park, Tom and I would continually meet up for runs, which was my saving grace. He acted as a life guide who continually pumped hope into the cavern of my heart. The moment was drawing closer. I had shared this decision with some friends and family who had a handful of doubts. I felt it necessary to clear the air before departing and penned a message to my family.

To Run

A Letter

As the weeks pass and the day draws closer to my departure for California, I find there is much to be said. If there is anyone in this world who I want to understand what my intentions are once I reach California, it is my family.

So where should I start? I guess the long of the story comes from my college years at Indiana. Running on a team at the collegiate level made my passions and dreams burn brighter than ever. I had people who understood me on all levels. Running is such a huge part of my life and if you don't understand that, then it makes it difficult to understand me. I made friends in college that knew me for 100% of who I was. They became an extended family. I now join hands with these friends as we embark on a new phase of all our lives. This trip was not the result of one person's ideas or goals, but the result of four people with unfinished business in the department of running.

I am going to California because it offers me a new environment where I can spread my wings and find myself. I want to explore different places and broaden myself as a person. I want to qualify for the 2004 Olympic Trials in the 1500 meters. That means I will make every sacrifice possible for that dream to come true. When in college, we went through a coaching change my junior year, and because of that, I could see my potential as a runner. The only problem was that I ran out of time at Indiana. I was stuck under the guise that I was an 800-meter runner. It was what I was comfortable with and therefore I continued to do it. I did not want to make a change so late in my career fearing disaster, but now I realize that a change is clear.

I taught in the fall of 2001, and once I learned to handle the load of teaching and coaching, I loved my job! It was midway through the cross country season when I became frustrated. I was trying to do what was best for the team, but my unfulfilled goals were eating away at me inside. I would watch these guys go out and race each week getting closer and closer to their goals all the while I was distancing myself from my own. It was then I decided that I was not done. I trained, but training with the guys while trying to fit in my own specific workouts was not compatible. I could not help others to the best of my ability until I answered the call of my heart.

In line with Josiah Gilbert Holland, I too believe that "the heart is wiser than the intellect"; intellect focuses on security while your heart acts on wisdom. Despite what society says I need to do to be secure and happy, I would rather trust my heart. Only I know what can make me happy. I then decided that I would finish out the year of teaching and move to Bloomington to work on my base training before I left for California in August. That is when things went awry at my job and my trip out-of-town came about faster than I had planned. I left my job in the first week of March moving to Bloomington two weeks later. At this point I needed an escape from the familiar surroundings of Illinois and Bloomington seemed ideal since some of my friends were still there and it would elevate my training level. I was crushed when things didn't work out at my job, but I was destined to make light of the situation and turn it into a positive.

Once I moved to Bloomington, things seemed to get better. I was running at a new level and I had the comfort of being with old friends who helped me separate myself from my most recent situation. I began to tutor for the University and received every endorsement possible from my old coach. Everything seemed to be falling into place. It was then that the seed was planted in my mind to write a book. My book is now 150 pages old, continues to be a work in progress, and another dream to conquer. I also had the intention of getting my masters. I had an ideal training environment with old friends and a school where I could get my masters. What else could I ask for?

Well honestly, for some time I thought it couldn't get any better. My training continued to go well, but then I fell into a hole financially. I wanted to be financially independent, but I just wasn't getting the work hours required. I didn't want to accept money from mom and dad, but I figured maybe it would just take one month and I would get back on my feet. Well, it didn't happen, and I quickly fell into a cycle of depression. My running suffered as a result. Normally there is always something going well in life and the focus turns to those things, but in this case, there was no light to be found. Running went downhill, I had little inspiration to write and rarely left the house. For a month, I locked myself away from society.

It was a very difficult time when Tom Brooks called and told me he was coming down to Bloomington; it did little to up my spirits. We talked about my situation as I alluded to my financial struggle and my training. My goals had all but washed away and I had no drive. His advisement was to get home and do whatever possible to reestablish some stability. At the conclusion of our final run he said, "Billish, let's chase that dream." We ran every day that weekend, and it was the best I had felt in a very long time. For the first time in over two months, I had a vision.

What I mean when saying I had a vision is that I had a mental image of my goal. Ever since my sophomore year of high school, I have always had an internal drive that resonated out of these sometimes fantastical thoughts. During runs it would appear, and my energy would explode. It was a feeling of elation that was unmatched. Those visions ranged from winning conference titles to state titles, and now that vision has me on the starting line at the 2004 Olympic Trials in the 1500 meters. The only thing that can match that feeling is realizing that vision. When the day arrives where it becomes clouded or disappears, my days of competitive running will be over.

The day after Tom left, my dream was reborn, and I planned to get home as soon as possible to get my life back on track. Now I am back in Palos and nine days away from taking one step closer to achieving my dream. What it comes down to is that I am not satisfied. I still have the fire in me to compete and feel if I don't take this chance, I will regret it the rest of my life. If I go out to California and I do not achieve all the goals I have set in mind, I will be upset, but I will be satisfied that at least I didn't sit around wondering what could have happened. When I am done with competitive running, I will have no regrets. Once this is out of my system, then I could move onto the next part of my life, whatever that may be.

I am certain that the number of things I can thank you for are too many to mention. You all mean so much to me and if there is one thing I regret it is that I did not take advantage of the time we had together. I will miss all of you dearly but know that you will always be with me in spirit. You will share the successes down the line and be the strength when things are not going to plan. I am very fortunate to have a family like I do. Whenever I talk to people about their families, some dysfunction exists, but all that came my way was constant love and support. I hope you all understand that I need to do this. I do not believe that California provides a utopian environment, although I believe that it offers me the best opportunity to advance my running and develop as a person. I do not know how permanent this trip may be; I will allow life to dictate that. T. S. Eliot once wrote, "Only those who will risk going too far can possibly find out how far they can go." This is my barometer test. I do not have a future itinerary, and I am okay with that. I can tell you that because of your love and support, whatever I may do or wherever I am living, I will be smiling.

Just Go!

The only person without a doubt resurfaced in my good friend Ryan. He asked no specifics about the trek west, but he said the one word that consecrated my journey's direction, "Go!" That was it! In its simplicity, so much more was communicated, and peace came from it. California was enticing for sure, despite me never having travelled that far west. The main encouragement was returning to my college teammates and just being together as we traversed this new road. Alongside Tom and I were two former roommates, Tom Chorny and Jon Teipen. Brooks and Teipen transferred their job placement to Los Angeles, Chorny was still attached to a professional contract and me, well, I was unemployed, yet fear of this decision was nowhere to be found. Jon found a place in Pasadena, a two-bedroom back house.

The trip began with the caravan arriving at my parents' house early on January fourth. Four cars occupied the long stretch of driveway with everything we cared to bring, no furniture, just the necessities. It was an effective purging to redeliver us to a life of simplicity. In route, we made stops in Oklahoma to get in a run and then a brief stint with another teammate, Eric Heins, in Flagstaff, Arizona where he was assisting the Northern Arizona University cross country and track & field teams. Flagstaff was a popular location for altitude training, and it was a common act for runners to take up residence there for short stints, simply crashing on floors of rented houses. With each mile of our new venture, every stop provided something unique...warm weather in January. The dismantling of our wardrobe continued as we hit Flagstaff. There was snow on the ground, but we were shirtless, quite the odd feeling. All our journeys were just beginning, and the excitement was palpable. Eric was prepping his next step to the Southeast Missouri State program where he ended up winning six Ohio Valley Conference Championships in just three years. A quick hop from there to a stint at TCU and then back again to Flagstaff where he guided the cross country team to its first national championship. The streak sits at three in a row. I continually encourage Eric to put together his remarkable story, but if interested in a summary, check Runner's World.

As Eric was traversing into the unknown as a head coach, the direction of my travelling party was less defined. Our time in Flagstaff came to an end as we entered the final stretch to our new lives in California. We rolled through the desert and were finally greeted by the San Gabriel Mountains. When we finally arrived, giant smiles encompassed our faces, and we began the walk down the long driveway which ended with the garage saddling our new housing complex. Quickly a decision was made to head to Walmart to garner the required things to get through the night including our beds (air mattresses) which stayed with us for years.

As we acclimated to our new environs, we explored the basis of our training: The Rose Bowl and NASA's Jet Propulsion Laboratory or what we referred to as JPL, Pasadena City College's track and the neighborhood loop encircling the California Institute of Technology (Cal Tech). In the coming days, Jon and Tom began their jobs, while Chorny and I were still figuring it out. Previously, I had reached out to my cousin Mike, who lived in Seal Beach. He opened the first door for me with a recommendation to a mom and pop running shop in Redondo Beach. After a quick call, I was employed and working alongside two former North Central College grads, one, a former national champion in the 1500. I began the commute daily as a new employee at The Village Runner, which was quite a haul coming from Pasadena.

Considering our lease was month to month, we decided to move once we were more familiar with the area. We settled in Santa Monica, blocks from the beach and a quick jog to Venice Beach. This two-bedroom establishment was nothing fancy and became crowded when all were home. We were seldom in the house which makes sense living in Southern California. This crowded space shrunk considerably with the addition of another former teammate, Chris Ekman. There was no lack for training partners as we covered the distance ranges from the 1500-marathon. When our schedules aligned, Team Indiana West was the result. We had all the support systems possible: meals together, rehabilitation, and a solid training team. Mostly, our home track was at Santa Monica Community College, the home of the infamous Santa Monica Track Club, although we ventured to UCLA occasionally. There was nothing quite like knocking out a workout while witnessing the HSI Track Club composed of the fastest men in the world: Maurice Greene, Ato Bolden and Jon Drummond, dousing each other with competitive banter. It resembled a team atmosphere with all the activity surrounding us. These outings unfortunately began to dwindle.

Time went on, life changed, and we all had consuming elements that disrupted the unity of our training. I was amassing hours at the running shop with Chris and opened the second location in Manhattan Beach. The diversity of our disciplines also changed as we moved closer to race specific training, which made aligning workouts increasingly difficult. Fitness progressed, but I began to be hampered by lingering injuries, not to mention my place in life was being altered. When I first arrived in California, my direction was singularly pointed, but now I was seeing the larger picture of the running shoe industry. This attraction cut into my training regimen and my focus was becoming clouded. As I continued to build relationships with the brands, opportunities began to surface. I worked with Adidas for the Los Angeles Marathon and was being exposed to the underbelly of this profession. Two significant moments began to reshape my thinking.

To Run

Divine Guidance

A friend of mine was hosting a guy by the name of Frank Shorter, an Olympic gold medalist in the marathon in the 1972 games in Munich who also won a silver medal four years later in Montreal. After some conversation, he signed my training log as we discussed my current situation and goals. Much came out of this dialogue as it was clear that I was not entirely happy with the results of my training. Conveniently, the one thing that could tell part of the story was my training log which just so happened to be the one item I had available for him to sign. He began scrolling through the pages and his expression was enough for an uncomfortable stomach drop. With continual nods of dissatisfaction, Frank started pointing out some glaring holes all the while stressing consistency in training. Here I was just some average Joe with the eyes of a running legend directed at my training. I don't know if I really understood how amazing it was that Frank Shorter was adding meaningful commentary to my training as I was more nervous about the next disappointing page for him to visit. It made sense why he had so much success; his everlasting scrutiny and attention to detail

175

were something I was duly lacking. My retort was subtle as the awareness of the fantasy turn nightmare rose from the pages. I would drop a gem of a workout only to be followed up by adjusted schedule training to compensate for work obligations then another hiccup. This pattern was not present to me prior to this moment. Strength over the years, season upon season, was the extent of Frank's utterings. What would it take for me to right the ship? I didn't have the answer, but this shadow around my training and intention became ever the more tangible. Because of my new work life, my training had taken a few bruises and the band aids were no longer covering up. This was not the nail in the coffin; however, it initiated a profound self-evaluation.

It wasn't too much time later that another messenger was delivered in the form of Bill Rodgers. He was the former American record holder in the marathon and had a phenomenal streak at the Boston Marathon, chaining together three successive victories. The surgeon quality of Frank was not noticeable in Bill, but one element was, pure joy. Although he was past his running prime, there was no lack of enthusiasm for the sport that made him a household name. In his laid back way, he made one thing clear, no matter what you do, be sure you love it... for you! Wow, now I was truly reeling, but my training continued. Do I love what I am doing? I wasn't sure, plus I had four roommates committed to the same thing. Was it about me or was it about appeasement? I had fallen into that state far too many times.

In a short period, I was graced with two renowned former professionals, but the major chip hadn't fallen yet. As alluded to previously, I tended to live in the wake of others, most notably my sisters and cousin Mike. When my cousin took a position at Brooks Sports corporate in Bothell, Washington, the West Coast Marketing position was vacated. I felt prompted to at least stick my head out there and see what would happen. As luck would have it, I landed the job. The fortunate part of the position was the allowance to control most of the scheduling, at least in visitation of my accounts. This was promising and could create a more positive circumstance for my training, so I remained optimistic. The boost of getting the position put some added energy into my training but with all new things, there was some adjustment.

The job required continuous travel not just in my region, but there was also the east coast marathon swing from Washington DC, New York to Boston. This is not me saying it was all met with drudgery as it was a running company and my travels included signature marathons. Despite the engrossing nature of my job, maintaining an edge in training was problematic. To add to it, living in California and the proximity to the beaches added a conflict. Throughout

To Run

college, barefoot running was a consistent element to my training, so why not use the beaches as I typically did the Billy Hayes Track infield? It just so happened to be the most convenient course as I was never far from a beach traveling up and down the coast. Without taking into consideration the pounding on hard, packed sand, I continued to extend my mileage on the beachfront. As an athlete, one of the most difficult things to do is understand when pain is necessary and when it is a cause for concern. Even though there was some pain in my Achilles, I backed off minimally. I no longer could do the heavy pounding of track workouts, especially spiking up, so I hit soft surfaces as much as I could.

Nail in the Coffin

As I became more consumed in my job, the battle of constant rehabilitation of a partially torn Achilles, and limited workouts caused much distress. Looking for some companionship on one of my trail runs, I recruited my roommate Chris in route to Penmar Golf Course, close to where we lived in Santa Monica. We were maybe five miles into the run when my legs just stopped, like that day in Bloomington. When Chris noticed me drop back, he asked if I was okay. My response caused no concern as I said, "I'm done." Chris double checked that I would be fine to make it home, as he continued. The message to Chris was that I was just calling it a day.

I can't quite explain the relief that came with those words passing through my lips. It was a reflective journey back home, just over a mile, but I never returned to a run, I walked and sighed. Could it be, 15 years from my entrance into the sport, it was now over? When I returned home that day, I still questioned myself, which was more a result of feeling like it would disappoint my teammates. Quite the contrary was the response. At the end of the day there was more respect in the decision than disappointment as everyone preferred honesty over imitation. The Olympic Trials came and went which initiated athlete flight. Switches in sponsorships and training groups were common since most runners had annual contracts. With retirement, this was not a concern to me. I finally felt like I had direction and was ready to embrace my role at Brooks Sports.

The adjustment to this new life was seamless, but what came next created some considerable alteration to my lifestyle. Brooks, Teipen, and Chorny headed for Eugene, Oregon, and Ekman shifted to Northern California to take on a sales gig with Adidas. With the shake up, I secured a place in Manhattan Beach with a different former teammate, but one who was not training. I continued my job and had some great opportunities to travel the country. I was a guest speaker at the Buffalo Run on Catalina Island, sponsored the Los Angeles Triathlon and Endurance Sports Awards, where I met some legends of cycling and triathlon and did not have to concern myself with fitting in training. Even though I really enjoyed my job, the absence of my close confidants created a gap that could not be filled. The only semblance of normalcy was heading up to Santa Barbara to crash with Aaron or up to Eugene to see the remaining mates. The unfortunate part was that these visits were not as frequent as I would have liked. Things were just not the same;

simple leisure hangouts no longer existed. The walls started to fall again. I began to question the relevance of my current lifestyle. I was not training for anything anymore, my social life was exhaustive and destructive, and my closest friend was two hours away.

To compound my situation, I ran into some financial issues. I was paying the brunt of the rent, roughly $3000 a month, which required me to pull money from other places not by choice. I was sinking and did not have the answer, nor did I have the relationships present daily to help ease the consuming doubt and fear. Brooks Sports continued to grow, and with it, new positions were opening at corporate. Many of my fellow marketing peers jumped at these opportunities, but I was not one. The battle in mind between "SoCal" or the "PacWest" and my fight with depression made it a no brainer, but the lacking intrigue of the place I called home didn't fill the cup either. It was time, this season had come to pass.

To Run

PART THREE
FALL

To Run

Where do I go from here?

Fall is my favorite season of the year aligning with the start of a new year, at least for a teacher. There are so many unanswered questions yet endless possibilities that sit before you. My soft spot may result from experiences that revolved around cross country and the transformative effect it had on me. It brought with it a new identity. Many view the fall as the end as most of us have been through schooling, and don't appreciate the summer escaping. I relish with the opportunity to hit the reset button and put all the dreams that surfaced in the summer months into practice. The resounding fear we face is change.

The move back to Illinois was the only thing solidly founded as what I would do upon my return was a mystery. I sought all options by whatever means possible. In the early stages of my search, what I wanted to do with my life was very much undecided, or better yet, not even near my thoughts or actions. I applied anywhere and for anything which landed me in sleazy door sales and college recruiting. Things were not syncing up the way I had intended and

185

the debt I had acquired in California continued to loom. I could not start this next chapter without a place to rebuild. My parents were more than helpful in many regards but moving home humbled me. The simple fact, I had no money. That meant turning down opportunities to go out with friends because I lacked the resources to grab dinner or a drink. My social life capsized as a result, but my focus remained on righting the ship.

With nothing fitting, something popped up, Velocity Sports Performance. It sounded in line with some things I was interested in, so I gave it a shot. From the outside, this appeared to be a dream job. I would work in a high caliber, athletic facility with anything and everything an athlete could desire. The only catch, I would not be on the floor doing the coaching, rather, in an office. It was my initial taste of the sales business. I had quotas, and I had a list of contacts. Cold calling, that was much of my job; it was brutal. I have never been one to force my views on others, especially when it was attached to finance. Even though I had a strong belief in the product, it was a burden asking people to pay for the services. If I had my way in life, I would mimic that of my late uncle and give it all away. If I feel that someone should have what I am offering, they will have it. This isn't the greatest way to be lucrative in such a business. The trend has continued even with this book although printing costs can be cumbersome with all the charity. Apparently, this was not the fit I was looking for, although it opened some doors.

No Longer a Runner

It was clear that I was not well suited for sales, but I stuck it out and eventually moved into a higher role as the marketing manager. This was a better fit for sure. I started to find my feet, enjoyed my job, but continually ran into obstacles. The most prominent of these was what money was coming in could hardly balance what needed to go out. The most important lesson I learned was to be vigilant with my finances. Working paycheck to paycheck was not ideal, as there was a constant in terms of unsettled feelings. One bad sales month, nothing to show for it. I needed to do something. I needed an idea, something I was passionate about to drive this business, then it hit me. I was a runner, one that, at times, lacked ideal training and facility. I have all of this now at my fingertips and it created the brainchild of Illinois Elite.

The impetus for the development of this program came from an evaluation of athletes who had been through the center that had an interest in running. It started small as expected with a crop of high school athletes. As one who does not fully support club running when the athlete has access to solid coaching, my mission was more creating unity within the running community. In high school, my team was rather small. When I would move on in the postseason, I seldom had company and the invitation to train with a local, rival high school surfaced. My community viewed this as anarchy and frowned upon it; I never saw the harm in it. I was offering something that was not offered elsewhere. My goal was not to take credit for a group of individuals' successes but to provide the means for the sport to grow. I would set up days and times for local runners to meet up and run with runners from other schools, aligning similar pieces of their individual training regimens. I was less a coach and more a logistics coordinator. It was always under the umbrella of making everyone better and changing perspective. As a coach, I have exercised this philosophy in the early stages of program development. I brought in former Illinois state champion and Nike Cross Country Nationals (NXN) champion, Sean McNamara, on one occasion. My only instruction to my guest was to hang out with the team. This action alone started to dispel the myth that elite runners were robots, lacking any feeling or doubt. Same went with the training. All the "big names" in the state were human as well and putting them in like company gave them more confidence. It erased doubts as they started to believe they could do what the other had done. I had to wait until I was in college to have this kind of insight and feel I could have benefitted from it sooner, when I was isolated from matching talent. This provided me connection into the running community around the Naperville area, a place foreign to me in the past. There was no attendance taken, no cost, just the chance to meet and run with others. It grew, about 40 runners took part. Their relationships with their competitors and performances accelerated. As I followed many of these athletes in their competitive seasons, the energy of the high school realm resurfaced interest in coaching, although I sidelined the prospect for the time being.

Around this time, I came into connection with Patrick Tomasiewicz. Patrick had run for York High School and, in conversation with many, was Coach Joe Newton's "go to", which I quickly learned why. He was a prodigy, for all intents and purposes, and his vision was remarkable. With the gap between the state meet and the Nike Track & Field Nationals, the goal was to provide another highly competitive meet for athletes to attain a qualifying time or another opportunity to improve on their state performances. It was the first meet of its kind, minus the national meet, where qualifying standards existed. In addition, it mimicked the European circuit in the provision of rabbits to get runners to their prescribed times. Patrick and Scott Bell authored the genesis of this event and were joined by me and Charlie Kern (York's current head coach). Their intentions lined up perfectly with my own; to create greater interest in the sport and provide new opportunities for runners that had not previously existed. The Midwest Distance Gala was born and fitting its institution was at the mecca of high school distance running, York High School.

The meet was organic and was built off relationships. The most notable in the early years was with a Jacobs athlete named Evan Jager: current American Record Holder in the 3000 Steeplechase and Olympic Silver Medalist. The primary focus was to get people to run fast and feel elite through meet function and treatment. It didn't take much beyond that as the master rabbit himself, Charlie Kern, took Evan to a lifetime best. The chips began to fall, and the notoriety of the meet launched, attracting not only the top runners in the area, but the country. It became the primary feed for Nike Nationals. Footlocker National Cross Country Champions joined the field and the marketing development exploded. In one of the final years, I was fortunate to host our first coaches' clinic, where we brought in Joe Newton, Jay Johnson, and other notables. It led to events such as the Brooks PR meet and the Adidas Dream Mile. It was innovative. This meet, along with my goal of bringing excitement to running, introduced me to the next facet of life.

Back to School

I can't say that something drove me to coach or to garner acclaim for building a program, but when I was humbly asked by a runner I had worked with in the summer to be his coach, I had to oblige. What this meant for my career direction was still blurry, so I maintained my role at Velocity and joined the coaching ranks at Marmion Academy, an all boy Catholic high school in Aurora, Illinois. The interview process was not what I would have expected. I cannot be sure there was an interview. All it took was a call from the athlete's parents, who initially presented me with this opportunity, to Dan Thorpe, the head track coach. It was a simple conversation that ended with, "Can you start tomorrow?" After checking in with my place of work, I made the arrangements that needed to be made. This meant, with the new endeavor, that my days would now stretch from 8 a.m.- 9 p.m. as to make up the time lost at work for practice. I was grateful for the accommodation of my employer and considering I was not in a relationship, this extension of my day was of little consequence.

To Run

I was barely into my first season coaching track & field, primarily with the distance squad, before another idea was circulated. "English teacher position opening, you teach English, should I put in your name?" was the utterance of Dan Thorpe. I was meshing with the community and felt it was worthwhile to at least see if that possibility existed. I had grown weary of my schedule of constant performance to earn a paycheck. It was the one thing that tainted my energy so to find something steadier was a wish. I was every employer's dream, someone willing to take a meager paycheck as long as it was the same each month. It would go a long way in helping me organize my financial debt payoffs. When interviewed for the teaching position, the panel asked me why they should hire someone who had been away from education and was in sales/marketing prior. I climbed onto the pulpit and declared that all stages of life involve sales and marketing to include education. I have a product and potential clientele, that through some form of enticement, I need to guarantee some return on investment. It was not the end of the world to me if I did not land this job, although the stain of Marmion on me clarified that despite my wants, this was God's want.

The Lord's intervention came first with the Grange family getting me in the door, and the other, Dan Thorpe. Dan advocated for me from day one. We built a strong relationship that went far beyond our individual sport. It is my belief that something united us to create a new culture, to challenge one another, and to grow in ways we never thought possible. To this day, I am indebted to him for all he has done and continues to do. My life was irreversibly changed, and it amazed me daily the storyline God continued to construct.

I always believed myself to be a man of strong faith but anything in my life to resemble that did not exist. Now that I was joining a Catholic community, I needed to sort it out. My faith went from a specific focus to more of a general idea in college. That idea, just be a good person. Who knows what that means, but that was my mantra for some time based on nothing concrete, so who was I to determine what good even was? I did not know how I would reform, but my life was about to change. The initial responsibility was to take on the challenge from the current members of the community to manage the freshman, something that had eluded a few previous teachers, and the one I was coming in to replace. I had a confident retort in these situations. My inner thoughts revolved around the gift I had been given, to relate and understand people that many others could not. They set the gauntlet which I believed could be conquered, but in the meantime, I had a season to focus on before I was to step in the classroom.

The first day of practice arrived, and I was unrefined in this discipline, leading a group of teenagers and applying years of knowledge to the training regimen. Despite these glaring weaknesses, I had some intangibles that came naturally: passion, challenge, and relatability. In my extensive research on the team, roughly 12 hours, I learned that state qualifiers and placers hadn't been a common trend in recent years. The group of guys assembled were aimless and not particularly motivated. We gathered for our first team meeting on the concrete steps of the track's back stretch, which became our natural meeting place for years to come. I programmed nothing for this speech, but once I was in front of the boys, the first utterance was, "Do you like to suck?" Fairly candid I know. I am reminded of this with my former runners whenever we reconnect.

The question I felt was necessary, although I believe with more time to prepare, it would have come out differently. From the beginning, my focus was on the collection of young men to do great things, but a lot needed change. I refused to spend a bulk of my time working with a group of individuals who would prefer to be elsewhere, so my unapologetic nature made our small team smaller. What happened, I took the recreation out of the team. I wanted them to see that there was a greater purpose in every step they took. We had a collective responsibility to contribute fully in all we did. The most basic message was showing up is not enough, it is a waste of talent and a waste of time. It resurrected my past teachings, and I felt responsible to do something that hadn't been done before while generating a culture of self-worth and collective worth. The small mass in front of me without a name would build a name and we would do it together.

In these days, minus relationships and a social life because of limited funding, running was my absolute number one. Practice was just the beginning of my day; the ensuing hours were laced with study and evaluation as I was learning to become a coach. I individualized everything and adjusted often. When I look back at some program design today, it was genius, if you call philosophies that didn't necessarily mesh genius. As any coach could attest, you learn by doing. I had a lot of learning to do, but my focus remained in one primary place, motivation. How could I make these endless miles seem worthwhile? How could I reprogram their brains in a way where they would challenge themselves? I wanted what we were doing to be owned by each individual. I could bark all day what I wanted, but this was a collective endeavor. My motivation was genuine in that I wanted these boys to see how good they could be although it did not reduce the level of intensity in my pitch.

As motivation became a key, a gift that had remained dormant since my time in college reemerged. I didn't grow the team with my own plans; I grew the team because I cared. Every relationship, every boy was a vital component to transformation. We had talent, but few dug into it. Most coaches will have that substantial talent show up from time to time and many invest 90% of their energies into said individual. Even though my arrival on campus was because of one specific individual's family, who was our top runner, he was no different in my eyes than the rest. I wanted the boys to stop focusing solely on themselves and learn to celebrate one another. For every good day a runner has, there are a handful worse days. My message was no matter the circumstance surrounding you, find a reason to celebrate. If a PR or race win were not in the equation for the day, find someone else who met one of those goals and raise them up. In the most succinct form, I challenged them to ask, "what does love require of me?"

This was the challenge, and it was not an easy thing for them to grasp; it taught me a lesson in patience. Despite my will to be instantly transformative, relationships were not something I could generate in short. They had to go from little to no motivation, and selfish driven attitudes to "another first" approach. Struggles ensued, but there was a patch of boys who truly bought in. With time, improvement and a new investment were being seen. We walked away with a conference title that year, which was nothing substantial, but it was just the beginning. Our shot at state surrounded two individuals, junior Josh Stein and senior David Grange. Josh was slated for the 3200 at sectionals joining David who would also contest the 1600. It was the 3200 where we had the best shot. Prior to this race, Josh had run 9:35 and David, 9:23. It was a deep field headlined by Neuqua Valley's Chris Derrick, so the assumption was that things would be taken out at an uncomfortable pace, considering our times going in matched with our competitors seed times.

The stage was set at Plainfield Central High School on a beautiful day for distance runners. Returning to a sectional, this time as a coach, did not ease the tension I felt. It was as if I was in the race with my boys. I nervously paced back and forth prior to the gun and then the rumbling of the shot blast was felt as I jerked back to trigger my stopwatch. Chris went to the early lead as expected and David sat on his shoulder. Josh was some way back, but a visual analysis was not accurate as this field was out quickly. Halfway home and Derrick broke the field, sub 4:30 through the mile. David sat in third position next to another Neuqua runner in Danny Pawala. This was a good sign based on how Danny had been running so my confidence in David was strong, but where was Josh? He was in a tangled mess of runners quite a distance back and I wasn't sure that this would be the day.

As the race was progressing, there was a lot of excitement as Chris had a shot to run sub nine minutes. My job at the meet was as the picker for the first place finisher, not ideal considering I had two horses in the race. The further Chris pulled away, the harder it was for me to see the development of the race. My attention drifted to the other task as Chris turned into the final straightaway. It would be close and as he broke the tape, the excitement of an 8:59.20 performance resonated. As I walked Chris off to the fence for staging, David was in sight pulling away from Danny to run 9:15, an 8 second PR. Josh still had a straight away to go. For the first time I looked down at my watch to see it eclipse 9:20 and there was Josh, 9:28 even. I had the same feeling most competitors have and the one I experienced in high school, once I locked my state slot, total release. Even though David still had the mile, his preferred event, now the tension was relieved from both of us and we prepped recovery to double back.

David, as Andrew Larson would mimic in my saying, was the "ultimate competitor." Questioning if he would show up in any situation was never a concern. He listened, did the work, but when the gun shot, what he had, no one could have given him. I really did not know what to expect considering he just ran a lifetime best roughly an hour prior, but when the race started, he resumed his typical position up front. He ended up winning in 4:18. The day was done with three state qualifiers. The celebration was short lived as the week leading up to state was one that frustrated me. My state athletes were not the source of this bitterness, more so the absence of a team to run and support them. This is what I wanted to build, a team concept despite qualifying a few individuals. To me, the season was not over. From my time in high school, once the postseason hit, I was often alone. I didn't enjoy it much as my head would gain too much control over me. We started the season together and my vision was we all finished the season together. I could do nothing at this exact moment, so I redirected my attention to Charleston, Illinois and Eastern Illinois University.

Whenever it came to state in the Thorpe era, he more resembled a loving parent than anything. He was selfless and planned to excess to make sure the boys had everything they needed. State was a different experience back in 2007. Phones had not matriculated into the mainstream, so state meets were more about camaraderie through conversation. It was a time of bonding that could not be replicated; we were one family. We consumed every waking hour with one another. With Josh running only the 3200 final on Saturday, Friday preliminaries were on tap for David in the 1600. As we entered the big blue oval, memories could not help but resurface from my final stand in Charleston 11 years previous, and my first return since. We headed to the check in tent surrounded by the orange weathering fence, exactly how I had remembered it. The tension became palpable as I recall my final entrance into that tent, but the hope was this would be the first of three visits for David. When you drop off an athlete at the tent, it resembles a goodbye; you no longer have any say or control of the events to come. It was another first for me as a coach as I played the role reversal of my last visit. I was not being left; I was the one leaving. The training wheels were off and now I was just another fan.

I found my way into the grandstand, front row at the top of the final straight. My goal is always to find an area with the least people in the hope to communicate with my athletes. This may have been my thought, but I should know from being an athlete myself, if you are in the right frame of mind, you hear nothing. My placement then was for me to think I was making some difference. Either way, I settled in as the Grange family joined me. Mrs. Grange, full of nerves after watching Evan Jager cruise a 4:13 to win the second heat, pried if I believed David could make it. It was shaping up in a way that David would have to run faster than he ever had (an improvement on his 4:15) to secure a spot in Saturday's final. Once the race got underway, she asked my opinion on his time and I said 4:13 confidently. I was equally nervous, but these words had no trace of doubt.

David's typical race strategy was to get out front, something he did not do on this day, which had me sweating while bolstering his parents. 800 meters in, he returned to his old form and sifted through the pack and sat tight on the leader. With this positioning, my doubts were erased because I did not feel there was anyone in his race with comparable leg speed. I looked intelligent as the last 400 unfolded and he charged to the lead finishing in 4:13.99, a lifetime best and the time I had predicted. It set a date with destiny, three state finalists.

With the talent of both fields, I asked David if he would prefer to focus on a singular race. With bold conviction he said, "real men double". I wanted to make sure that the decision was his and felt if he sat out the 3200, he had a shot at a title in the 1600. Many athletes would jump at such an opportunity. Jager was doubling, why wouldn't he? He wanted no unfair advantage; he just appreciated testing himself. It was never about a place or time, just challenge. The decision was made final, and we prepped for the 3200. With both in the same race it made scheduling a lot easier, not to mention, having a warmup buddy and partner in the ever dreaded check in tent. My job was done as I transferred the boys into the officials' hands, and I took my designated spot in the stands. As was the case a day earlier, I comforted the Granges with my prediction of 9:08. At this point I am not sure where I was pulling these times; maybe I was learning something based on workouts and potential. David was one of the easiest athletes I have had in terms of time prediction. The main reason was he raced every time, no mental blocks, no lacking confidence, just pure determination and focus. The field was star studded, including the likes of current national stars in Evan Jager and Chris Derrick. This would be a tightly contested match up... and fast.

Jager had the senior advantage on Derrick rattling off an 8:52 to 8:54. David finished a solid 5th in a time of 9:07.32. Josh came home in 9:26. Merely an hour later, David ran his second PR finishing fifth once again in the 1600 with a 4:13. The season was now complete, but the true test was yet to be seen as the next stage would happen in David's absence. As many solid athletes I have coached, I credit one person with their success and that is God. I may tweak something here and there, but these boys would have success wherever they went. The key is what happens when your talent graduates. This was a pivotal time. The program could be erased from memory and remain irrelevant; that was not on my agenda.

Starting to Build

I had survived my first full season at the helm despite my unrefined manner. My behavior and expectation were bold as I looked to disrupt the current of the past. I challenged everything: commitment to team, self, school, and sport, but one primary element contributed to the greatest transformation and it began within me. Throughout my life, it has been clear I cannot read into someone's thoughts or the depths of that person's mind, but I could see past the fixtures of the false self. What was revealed was the understanding of what I needed to provide each individual. Some required a stern challenge, others, endorsement of confidence. There is inherent worth in all of us and though we may not see it, it exists, and it is waiting to be uncovered. I have been given a wonderful gift of seeing behind the curtains to the struggles of my fellow man and though the variance of revelations makes it difficult to explain in elicit detail, it continues to be accessible to me. These barriers to achievement for my students and athletes I felt was my calling. There were things in life I was specifically designed for. I did not always understand my uncanny ability to relate to people of all walks of life, although my purpose was becoming clearer. Saint Paul conceded to God's plan with the simple utterance of "Let me do everything you wish". It was no longer my ship to sail, so I turned over the reins.

At this time, I began dating my now current wife, Renee. We had met through a friend and my roommate, Emily. My initial introduction to my bride took place at a women's shelter in Chicago. Renee led devotional time with these women; it was the purest, most beautiful thing I had witnessed. I was amazed at her tenderhearted nature. Joining this group brought back the yearning of service in me. This is not how I used to spend a typical Saturday night, but it was so much more rewarding, and it deeply fed my soul. My ability to commit to a relationship was not a priority as I invested so much time into my job, but our friendship remained. It was not for over a year that we fell into dating when God hinted to both of us that the timing was right.

One Question

My journey in self-exploration began with one question: "What is your relationship with God?" It was a struggle to define my relationship, but it was enough to move the chains. Renee popped this question amidst a picnic I had titled the "Morality Meal". It was in an attempt to get to know one another better; with each piece of food came a question that would further open us to one another. I created the picnic outing and therefore all the questions were of my doing. It was not until we consumed the meal, and all questions expired that Renee served the desert in the most redefining way, one question. This is all it took and the answer seeking began. I first believed that I had the answer, but as I continued to fumble through word after meaningless word, it became clear to me. If I could not answer this simple question, then my relationship with God wasn't what I had thought it was. My search continued as I sought church members, old friends, and literature. The acknowledgement of my faith was overwhelming, an increasingly heavy weight. I have always been a person who could not rest until I found an answer, and in this case, I committed every waking moment and restless night of sleep to resolving this question. The next week was inspiring as the Holy Spirit began to intervene in my life.

There is an email that remains in my Inbox even though it was written 12 years ago. It was a message blanketed to authors and clergy. The writing of it was unconscious, but after pushing send, I revisited what I had constructed. It appeared almost foreign, divinely inspired. The final sentence read, "I just want to go home!" Clearly this was not about moving back in with my parents or to my old neighborhood. Pat Conroy nailed my feelings exactly in his book, *The Lords of Discipline*: "I could not quiet that pearly ache in my heart that I diagnosed as the cry of home". The dawning of a new day came as I finally understood that my search was about a relationship with God. Every chance meeting or activity prompted me to ask, "What is God going to unveil to me through this?" My life seemed adequate to this point, but now I knew why I felt stale. After a large dose of soul exposure, my heart was racing. The most logical solution to my giddiness was a run. About two miles in, the knots of emotional burden initiated by the question lost their tension, which literally stopped my legs. I was awestruck and consumed; the tears rained down my face. The words of Soren Kierkegaard filled my mind's space and I mumbled, "Now, with God's help, I shall become myself". There was nothing sad about this moment. It produced so much joy that in looking to the sky, I knew I had arrived at my answer. I was teaching my boys about recognizing their gifts, but I was a mere voice, not the picturesque model. The swift transformation led to all acts being devotional in nature. I started to live the message I was delivering. God kicked the door down resulting in a tremendous energy. No longer did I believe in chance or luck, but purpose. My actions and words became divinely guided.

I used to always question where my answers came from even though the general assumption was that they came of my power or per chance. After some time under the misnomer of being self-sufficient, I detached from where the answers came from. To be honest, I felt like I had no answers, only questions. Through my faith journey, I now know where my answers come from. The responses never come in the same format, rarely heard but understood. Sometimes my answers came through responses from nature reflecting God's beauty. Other times through people who seemed programmed as messengers answering questions they never knew were asked. I abandoned the "self" as I began to lean on God and purely ask. My prayers were not in line with simple requests; I prayed big. My asks were not for things like hoping that the police officer I whizzed by did not catch me genuflecting at that stop sign. I asked to be made new, to usurp the old dilapidated version for a fresh model. The endless bounty of questions lessened and with these answers, I found something, myself.

Amazingly, the search for this answer opened my life and changed my way of thinking, not to mention my behaviors. As a coach and teacher still in his infancy, I was hard-nosed and direct. My intentions surrounded success, but that definition was altered. This spark led me into all kinds of readings on life and faith, but the most notable kick came from John Ortberg. In his book *Life Changing Love*, he addressed my prior shortcomings in that, "In isolation love dies; humility and compassion and generosity of spirit all suffocate". My purpose was to be directed outward, but I had to prepare my heart for the awesome responsibility. I redirected my time from constantly crunching numbers and evaluating competition to prayer and Bible study. As a teacher, my study hall supervision was now consumed with scripture and devotionals instead of analytics or simple time wasting. I began to pour myself into my boys and developed relationships far beyond my coaching and teaching responsibilities. I learned how gratifying it was to be a parent. All my kids, though most have transcended into adulthood, became another family to me. If it was not for the buy in of my original group, whatever plan I had would have fallen flat. Thank you to my first children: Oscar, T.J., Zack, Chris, Ben, Pat, Joe, Alex, Andrew, Matt, Bennett, Eddy, Ryan, Austin, Danny, Brian, David and Josh. I am never an empty nester as a coach. What I learned is that the most important aspect in life is relationship. After my first few years at Marmion, I knew every student in the building. I visited the cafeteria daily during my off period just to have conversations with the students.

To Run

I would not say I was a master recruiter or that I used guilt to get boys to come out for the team, I expanded my relationships. The numbers skyrocketed, and my band of 20 athletes now looked like a small army. The blessings continued to come. Once the numbers were elevated, management was becoming a concern. Conveniently, one of my current athletes said that his dad would join in if need be. I had little idea who this man was but expressed comfort brought Chuck Strohmaier into my life. As luck would have it, another athlete's parent also reached out. There was no interview process, just God's approval; the staff grew to three with the addition of Tim McLean. To call them volunteer coaches was a gross understatement. Volunteer to me means freedom and convenience; they would have none of it. They embedded into the fabric in a truly meaningful way creating roles and ways of doing things that never crossed my mind. I believe in angels now as there was no question that these men were there to help guide not only me, but all the boys. I saw it as role model overload.

With the addition of these men, the transformation was great. Having had handled the entire program by my lonesome in the past, I wasn't sure how to dole out responsibility and frankly, felt a little guilty asking these volunteer parents to take on any such burden. I wasn't even sure they would stick around beyond the time of their sons' graduation. The natural flow of responsibility just

happened. Tim became not only our legal eagle as the lawyer of the bunch but also the "race predictor," calculating mid race our positioning, for the most part, accurately. Tim also graduated from Marmion and was on the last state team, which was an added perk to help understand the history. Chuck was "Mr. Resource" as he had a knack to find anything we needed; a man that could get things. He reminded me of the character Red from one of my favorite movies, *The Shawshank Redemption*. In addition to another former coach in Tom Choice, who compiled meet by meet progression documents, we turned into a well-oiled machine in a short time.

The message delivered from all of us was the same. We were men of faith with the ultimate goal of developing strong men of character. We wanted to see the program grow and compete on the state stage, but we put even more time into developing well-rounded individuals who challenged themselves toward self-improvement no matter the arena. Not only was I blessed with these three additions as coaches, but they became mentors, confidants and friends. I will always cherish the time we spent together and what we were able to accomplish. As the head coach, my name may have been more visible to the outside world, but I would have never developed as a man or coach without the guidance and example they provided.

Peace Be Still

There was no time in my life that faith had become so integral in all that I did. The program continued to grow as we rattled off three consecutive Regional championships in cross country and a Sectional track & field big class win leading to a top 10 finish at the state meet. Even though the talent had turned over, the confidence in another state run remained. To saddle all of this, the school continued to undergo a transformation of its own. With the addition of Kurt Becker, a former Chicago Bear, incumbents Kevin O'Connor, varsity soccer coach, Bill Schalz, varsity swimming coach, and the continual encouraging push from head football and track coach, Dan Thorpe, individual teams began to disappear as we all became one unified collection of parts. We streamlined ideas and the support for one another was unmatched. We elevated no team above another. It is the only time in my athletic and coaching career I have ever seen such seamlessness. The coaches supported one another in attendance at events with a genuine interest in each other's success. I refer to this time as the golden era of my career as the coaches' model led to a trickle down to the athletes erasing discipline hierarchy.

To Run

Pep rallies converged, and credit to Dan Thorpe for removing the standard of it being only a football event, involved the inclusion of all sports. Despite the football team having a miraculous season, one that would warrant elevated treatment, it did not happen. One of the clear indications of this happened weekly as different sport teams would interfere with one another's practice to give high fives after a good win or words of encouragement after a difficult loss. This reciprocation came in a big way and is one moment of my career that cannot be erased from memory. It was the week of the state meet and we were having a team meeting on the concrete bleachers, my back facing the football field. I continued my inspirational speech or rant, can't quite remember what it was about because my athletes' distraction kept pulling me away. When I was about to lose it because I believed we were not focused, the boys signaled me to turn around. I turned to address the distraction; what stood before me was marvelous. The entire varsity football team was lined up from one end zone to another. Before I could question the purpose, Coach Thorpe started the greeting line. Our team walked through this line where heartfelt hugs accompanied dialogue of well wishes. It was the classiest event I had ever witnessed. It brought me to tears as I watched the rest of my team continue down the line. The authenticity of exchanges made me treasure the power of sport as the relationships established continue to exist to this day.

I know no other action that could have prepared us for our final meet of the season. Whatever message I was trying to send was delivered by the football team. It provided the peace I needed as we were heading into a race where the lineup was yet to be determined. In years past it was clear cut and the meeting night before race day was some motivational talk, distribution of numbers, and off to bed. Fortunately for us, we had arrived early and dropped by the course around noon. The rest of the day was wide open, which ended up being required for the decision we had to make.

Upon return to the hotel, the coaches gathered to mull over who would make up our top seven. The dialogue left us indecisive and it would require another step. We agreed that we would talk to the boys in question and see where their heads and hearts were. We asked them, "Why should you be included in the lineup?" I don't really know what we expected to get out of this since both responses were what a coach would like to hear; they had every confidence in themselves to make an impact. It was back to the drawing board. We let the situation breathe the rest of the afternoon as I devoted much time in prayer to make the right call. I then dropped in with each of the two boys and was transparent that this decision was not an easy one.

After dinner, things were still not sorted out, so the coaches convened one more time before the full team meeting. We decided to put senior Eddy Grahovec in the lineup. He was selfless and earned his spot. There was no question what he would contribute the next day, but there was a ceiling. The junior who we had foregone had a greater upside with an opportunity to crack the top five and really help us out if anyone faltered. His past racing; however, looked like an EKG chart and consistency was a concern. About thirty minutes before the full team meeting, the senior asked if we could talk. The contents of this conversation revolved around him surrendering his spot for the good of the team. It absolutely blew me away, but it cemented the decision, and all were on board. His willingness to sacrifice for the team was definitive of his character; I had promised that his day would come, and it did. Later that year, he pulled off the most unique double at a state meet I had ever witnessed: the 300 hurdles and 800 meters achieving All-State status in both. There was no more gratifying conclusion to his storybook career. Unfortunately, there was no way to know if his day would come, or if the last minute line up switch would prove correct.

It was now time for the team meeting and God laid a piece on my heart, Psalm 46:10: "Be still and know that I am God; I will be exalted among the nations, I will be exalted in the earth." I revolved my talk around this passage and the Holy Spirit did a work in me and that room. We shared hugs and whatever happened the following day could not compare to the unity we shared at that moment. In years prior, we had squads that had a handful more talent than the crew we were fielding, but our confidence in who we were and what we thought could happen were high.

We arrived at Peoria's Detweiller Park and the nostalgia came upon me. When I was younger, I visited this site often when my sisters and their team had qualified for the state championships. It was a special place and one I vowed to return to myself as an athlete. The vision of me bringing a team here was euphoric. I relived my meager performances as an athlete here as we warmed up on the course, but despite my poor showings, the special feeling remained. I decided at this point to keep the glory of Detweiller by only returning when I had a qualifier. Things had changed a little as the awards were no longer held at Peoria High School. It was like a grand ball back then. Athletes would shower and dress to the nines before being introduced as All-State members. I always wanted to join them, but it never rang true in my career.

Race day arrived, and we executed our typical routine since we had mimicked it earlier in the year at another meet on this course. We met one last time at the starting line, prayed, and they excused coaches from the starting box. As my typical routine, I head to a remote part of the course to communicate with my boys, but also because my nerves are equally high, and it provides me an opportunity to settle myself. My wife joined me on this trek as she was in attendance supporting her Naperville North girls. The race began and just over a mile in, I had extreme doubt as our positioning was far from what we had discussed. If you ask my wife, I was almost frantic. The race continued, and it appeared the only progress being made was our number one, Ben Kanute. Even though he was in All-State position, I had believed he would have been even further to the front.

I was far enough away from the finish to temper myself before being confronted with my athletes who I assumed would be surrounded by codling parents. My demeanor had to be checked; I needed to accept the outcome even if it was not up to my expectation. When I entered the box, while the athletes gathered their belongings, I could not escape the smiles on their faces. What had happened? Was I watching the wrong race? As the boys ran to me and hugged me, I thought this was a bad Twilight Zone episode. Once they relayed their times, my confused manner allowed me to join them in celebration as most of them had run lifetime bests, not to mention, our last-minute line up decision ended up being our number four. So, this was it, I had to be pleased considering the race was faster than most expected. The roadmap designed leading in did not connect with reality, but it also did not match up with other teams' objectives. One of my assistant coaches, Tim McLean, the scoring savant, predicted our placement, a lot closer to the podium than I would have thought.

Now I was really messed up as I went to the scoreboard to await the team scores. This was the slowest time had traveled in my life. My main goal was to inch closer and closer so I could secure a good glance before escaping the corral. The official with the flapping pages of results began his journey toward us. Coaches got antsy, robbing my space as they bounced me back and forth. The first thing posted were the individual results, not something I was particularly interested in. The pushing continued as eyes and phone cameras encroached. There was nothing left but the team results. My eyes were already positioned to the top of the board so I could gather the information as quickly as possible to avoid suffocation. I had a visual and detected a number three next to our name. This required a double take before I could return to camp with the news. My childlikeness arrived as I sprinted to our camp with shouts of "we took third, we took third". Hard hugs, tears, and an ultimate peace arrived. It was the first cross country trophy in the school's history and the celebration began. Once I had some moments with my team, I made a call to our head football coach to share the news and to wish them luck in the state playoffs that afternoon. That is what was built, sharing in our successes.

What happened after state very much resembled an NHL team winning the Stanley Cup. We transported this large physical structure to the team gathering after state, open house the following day, home with coaches, and eventually, presentation to the student body and Headmaster. The school put on a pep rally for the team where the football team created a path for my athletes to walk down upon entrance to the gym. This loving corridor hid us from the large monument set before the student body, where each boy was presented a laurel wreath. The parading continued at the Fall Sports Convocation and took us through December. It was an exhausting process, but I was glad to see how these boys were celebrated.

Trophies Rust

It was a whirlwind and time whizzed by. Then came Sunday morning, on a weekend the team had just gathered and spent an evening together. I received a call from one of my senior captain's parents. The news quickly erased the speed of life as I was confronted with the reality that one of my boys had passed. I was absolutely stunned, and all I wanted to do was to accommodate the family requests as much as possible. They asked me to serve as a pallbearer at his funeral to which I conceded not knowing how I could even stomach such a task. I owed as much to the family, his teammates, and friends. Attending the wake, the reality of it all began to sink in. I spent most of my day at the funeral home checking in with students and families. It was important for me to be surrounded by those in a similar circumstance as the shared experience made the reality more tolerable. I was afraid to return home alone to battle these demons head on.

The next morning, I was to meet at the funeral home before heading to the church for the funeral service. It was now nearly empty and eerie after being ballooned the day prior with the many lives he had impacted. I gathered with the pallbearers and family as we said goodbye for the final time. As we made our way to the all too familiar Marmion Abbey Church, the reason for our visit would be the last. A place we had shared for four years, now vacated of one. My eyes were foggy and mind clouded, which were even more tainted by the cold and snow as we escorted the casket into the church. The service was a stretched period that allowed us all to be together with the inevitable separation looming. The final journey to the cemetery I was numb. I drove in utter silence all day as I was hoping for some peace or comfort to be delivered, yet it never arrived.

I pulled into the cemetery and the tent marking our destination came into view. The temperature did not cooperate; as we stood next to the hearse, my face froze, trapping the emotion. We stood graveside where the harsh weather copied my response to the situation. I was about to bury my athlete, part of my family, my son! The blame came quickly in my decimated state, it was hard to resist. I wished I took specific opportunities, that I could have detected the persisting issue, but I didn't. This guilt was a burden, but the reassurance from his parents delivered peace. From this experience, it finally drove me to evaluate the depression I had always believed I could conquer. My perception of this part of my life being a weakness or more potent, a failure of my doing, began to change.

Mental health initiatives still came with a stigma and were not as prominent as they are today. I always was a believer in self-sufficiency, but when I experienced the power of mental illness firsthand, it was something that could no longer be ignored. The question that repeated itself in my head was how close did I come? The answer may have not been what I was looking for followed by the prospective question, could I be in that place again? My depression was a trap, something I had an inability to escape myself. Fortunately for me, God sent aide at the times I was at my lowest, when I questioned my place in this world. As a teacher, the emphasis of self-value and perception is something I repeatedly drill in the devotionals I lead my students in daily. I didn't want more statistics; I was now pushing toward awareness.

What happens after such an episode? Many times, the answer is far too predictable, resume life as usual. This would have been a tremendous failure. Something had to come from it, so I began the workings of mental health education which involved visits from the National Alliance on Mental Illness (NAMI) and some curriculum reevaluation. One of the greatest initiatives was taken on by another one of my athletes, Ben Minnis, who created an event he named "Party in the Park" to bring about awareness to the mental health issues plaguing society. In four years, he raised over $32,000 for Suicide Prevention Services of America. The stain of this event remains on my heart, but it also provided the therapy I needed to make adjustments in my life. The address of my mental illness included a complete reversal of thought. I am not self-sufficient, and I do not have the power to override my depression, but with additional support, depression no longer rules me. Losing someone I cared for deeply saved my life.

PART FOUR

Winter

To Run

So, Now What?

The season of winter is one that is often associated with death, darkness, hibernation, but I now see it differently. To me it has become a time of digging into the depths of life, re-birthing myself for what is coming next. I may hibernate to some extent, but that time is often filled with opportunities for me to grow through challenge of thought. I am a reflective person, but sometimes finding the time to do such a thing is elusive. When responsibilities lessened, I bore myself into advancement. The only death that takes place here is the death of an old self. C.S. Lewis eloquently puts it into perspective: "The seed dies to live".

I am not perfect, but I am ever evolving. Despite my past creating some barriers, I have learned to let go. Even though revelations have come from my disrupted beginnings, I am not immune to imperfection and failure. This ability to thrive amidst adversity came from a singular place, a deep-rooted trust in God. In Him I found myself. For so many years, I lived a life under a false self, trying to mold myself into the ideal image. This may have pleased others to a degree, but it left me empty. After years of continual failures and dark spaces, I came upon the antidote. I would never be the man I was designed to be living in this dystopia. This world controlled me, leaving my contribution null.

To grow our energies and purposes, we cannot depend on societal constraints. It is a trap that yields no fruit. Having momentary peace was not what I was out for, I was seeking a lasting peace. All of this was not possible until I took a stand and let the old self die. It took time for certain, but progress continued to be made. Once I fell into teaching, I knew I had found a home. Sometimes it is as simple as that, be where you belong. For too long, I was forcibly placing myself in positions I did not fit in. In looking back at the first disciples, they were master fisherman, but when the Messiah entered and filled their nets instantaneously, they aborted their life work to follow Him. To bring it into its most basic form, Jesus did what they couldn't do in ten hours, in ten minutes. Not a bad argument for bringing God into your life. The requirement does not call you to drop everything and meander around the earth blindly. Every job/career is a vocation. Work where you work and serve where you work. My career choice made motivation easy to find. I wanted to be there, and I knew I had to be there. This was my window; this was my environment for transformation.

To Run

A task I take on weekly, mowing the lawn, never seemed so insightful. Our front lawn is well manicured. I spend a lot of time making sure it is without a weed, patchless and overall presentable. The same does not ring true out back. What has come of our backyard aligns more with a jungle. We do not use the space that often, and therefore it offers more time for neglect. Weeds, and I mean some serious weeds, push out the lush lawn. I can only blame myself as I gave up on the back. The same is true in life; we spend an inordinate amount of time making sure our outside image is perfected but internally we rot. If you drive by our house, it looks great. If you venture beyond the front, another world awaits. I had a lot of weeds growing and it was time to pull them. My inattention to myself could have had grave consequences. The solution required calling in reinforcements.

One of the glaring commonalities in my times of despair was independence. Most would view this term in a positive light, but for me, it was a separatist movement. I may have been in the presence of others, but I was not in commune. This is one thing people can be ignorant of. Someone who suffers from depression may still be seen in the general sense, but they are as secluded as ever. I held onto anything of value and shared little of my plight. I am an introvert by nature and the amount of energy it requires for me to ramp up for social interaction often will leave me with little in the absence of company. This created quite the conundrum, as when in my space, the path my mind would travel often proved detrimental. I did not know how to balance this heavy flow of emotion, and with all of it bottled up, an explosion was imminent.

What I had to say about myself was hardly glamorous. The context was askew as my vision of myself blossomed out of a lacking relationship. I ran from relationships in the personal sense, but it was a spiritual relationship that required attention. Fortunately, my time in solitude offered a benefit. I spent a lot of time tangled in the text of books. These less than ideal situations functioned in the positive as they opened my heart and mind and began to present opportunities for advancement. Sometimes the transference of perspective opens us to a new way of living. We can get stuck at certain times in our lives, but opportunity always exists.

It is a hard pill to swallow as we prefer to feel as if we are hopeless causes and there is nothing that can retrieve us from the wallowing depths of our situation. Changing one thought at a time yields tremendous benefit. Sometimes I would view an encounter or event as displeasing, but what if I approached it as a possibility instead of a responsibility? What if work was not something I had to do to make ends meet, but use it as a catalyst to advancement? I started to take this approach by repeating the question: What is God going to teach me in this situation? This was my form of positive self-talk, and it worked. My job on Earth is simple, to love. My greatest weakness has become my greatest strength. Traveling my days has led me to one place, relationships matter, and my quality of life depends on them. Every day I come alive and sometimes interactions are reciprocated, but when they are not, I bleed my energy to that void. I want to be a guaranteed smile, high five, a slice of humor or compassion to whoever is set in my path. That is my calling, that gives me life. There are moments in life that entrance us. Through time spent in scripture, one of the most powerful lines that resonates with me is from Isiah 43: "Because you are precious in my eyes, you are honored, and I love you." I cannot explain the power that accompanies the final phrase, "I love you", coming from the creator of all things. I have found no greater joy than in knowing whose I am.

It is a simple equation, take on every challenge presented, but along with it, bring God. Some things may not have had a particularly positive outcome as I would see it, but all my interactions were preparation. If we view our lives as a big athletic contest, the one thing we see is that the continual training, sometimes modified, prepares us for something greater. This loss will eventually lead to this victory. We are all disciples in a sense, it is just a question of discipling to what outcome? Who are we serving, ourselves or others or even things? Where do we allot most of our time and energy? It is a basic benefit cost analysis. What I value is what I commit myself to. It can be a sad reality once we learn the reason of our frustration or pain and most of it is what we think we are doing in contrast to what we are doing.

Life is all about interruption. What we feel is interrupting us can tell us much about what is valuable. Is it a family party, school, work, or even the church that make us cringe? It is easy to set our path, minus any distraction; the quintessential perfect world scenario. The only problem here is that we don't live in a perfect world and our initial plans will be diverted or even cancelled. Dreams may die, but dreamers do not. Once the moment of question arrives, we must take swift action. Are we going to accept derailment or lay a new track? We can always question the "why's" in relation to circumstances we would prefer to discredit, but without momentary disorientation, growth is lost.

Conflict is life-giving even though society would say it is something we need to rid ourselves of. As an English teacher, a quick mini lesson here on plot line development. All stories have conflict, but it does not make them any less interesting; it does the opposite. We love to see the underdog rise. It is the accumulation of conflict that leads to a climax and ultimate resolution. Each week we go through hundreds of these mini life plot lines. Have you ever had a supposed failure turned around in time? My entire life is in response to my failures. They are the pieces that have constructed the man here today writing these words. Stop viewing conflict as a bad thing and instead learn to use it as an object of propulsion. See your injustices as a way to prove something. God puts difficulty in our life not to make us miserable, but because He knows we can handle it, and it is part of the refining process. Trial by fire is the common saying, and the routine nature of humans requires fire from time to time. We are not only saved from the fire, but it is the fire itself that we are saved by.

Life can be established based on different levels of inconvenience. We always have a way we would prefer events to play out and avoid all unnecessary disruption. But what if inconvenience was necessary? A whisper, hinting, or divine appointment? Continually viewing life in this way will, more than likely, change your circumstance in a powerful way. The amount of times something has pulled me out of my comfort zone are many and remain the most rewarding and transformational parts of my life. Maybe I did not want to wake up that early, take that trip, or initiate that conversation. Give me my inconvenience; it was worth it! If you want to evolve and transition from season to season you better be ready to adjust.

If I continue my yard analogy, the art of pruning is necessary for sustentation and growth of the plants and bushes that occupy the spaces surrounding my house. We prune a lot of things. I am not sure about you, but when I sit down to eat my morning banana, I do not eat the peal. I pull it away to get to the good part as I do with oranges. When our favorite shirt does not fit anymore, we can squeeze ourselves in it or get a new shirt. The applications are many, but we don't just prune the bad, sometimes, we need to get rid of some good. Based on the title of this book and the pages within, it is obvious that I love running. With each passing year; however, I have become much slower, deal with injuries and what not, but I still love it. I must cut mileage, diversify my training and possibly remove some of those lofty racing goals, but I do. When I left competitive racing, it was difficult for me to coach, because I was still in racing mode, not coaching mode. At some point, I needed to disengage on one dream to start the next. It is a season, and when a season ends, no matter how difficult it may be to surrender it, we must move on to the next season.

Anytime we question our direction, circumstances dealt us, or our purpose in this life, know one thing: Your story is part of the greatest story ever told by the greatest author of all time. Conflicts will arise, you will take your bumps and bruises, but as God governs out of mercy, you will see your rainbow. Today I am a shell physically of what I used to be, but my longing to run remains. There is something freeing about getting to run. My story began in disharmony, or at least that is how I viewed it, but it is just another chapter in a masterpiece. Running provided the setting of my life's journey, and it has been a wonderful teacher. I may not always enjoy the instruction, but I know that my best interests are at the center of it all.

To Run

Becoming ME

What is the secret to life? Most would list out activities to be involved in, colleges of attendance, profession, even the neighborhood in which they live. There is a plan for all our lives. We can live to fulfill another's wishes and have all the material possessions possible, but we will not find the answer there. I would like to say that I live without regret, but that would be false. I am human, just like the rest of you. I have failed, miserably, but I don't want a do over. Many of my decisions have created pain, some could have changed the landscape of my life. There is no way of telling what that would have looked like. All you get is what sits in front of you. The construction of this book was therapeutic. It brought shadows of my past to light, which allowed me to let go and turn that setback into a comeback. The most amazing gift was to step back from my life and see how majestically this storyline has been brought together. Every thread, some longer than others, some worn out, all came together to create me. The most vital part, the construction is nowhere near complete. I am living my story. You are living a story that has never once been told.

To Run

No matter societal comparisons to leverage ourselves or to bring more acclaim to our lives, life plagiarism is not only wrong, it lacks reward. I devoted half of my life to this kind of existence and what I learned was, that is not me. Happiness comes not from duplicating a mold but in sculpting your own. I am no longer consumed with how I am viewed from a superficial standpoint. I do what brings me life and provide a glare to those I surround. It is not a complicated science equation; it is the quintessential necessity of life. The most basic, but also the most difficult thing to do, love. Whatever life discipline consumes you, this is something that can be applied. You need not be the best at what you do, but you need to be the best version of you. Your impact is not based on wins or losses, sales, or title, it is based on someone finding something in you that brings them life. This is the life we were called to. Give of yourself for the benefit of others, that is love.

We can complicate matters quite frequently because our focus is broad. In any given situation, simply ask yourself, what does love require of me? That's it. It does not matter what sits in front of you, this question can align you with the proper perspective to make meaningful change. Our storylines are incredibly complicated which may lead us to believe the answer to the previous question is illogical at best. Don't fall into that trap of following the path of comfort. Nothing happens in comfort. We have all been given a spirit of love, it is the one constant that human beings share. This commonality is intentional, but we must align ourselves to it. People become so accustomed to saying "no" because saying "yes" creates a space of unknown. I love predictability as much as the next person although I don't recall transformation or extreme joy coming out of the expected.

"The path less travelled" is the token cliché that is the centerpiece of dynamic stories. From my time in California, I learned to love surfing. The early stages were quite unsettling as the grand abyss before me was "unpredictable". My imagination created visions of shark attacks or jelly fish stings. Despite these occurrences taking place seldom, they shaped my mind. I was afraid to leave the shallow water. Basically, my experience was that of anyone else who ever stepped on a beach, it was common. If I were to tell people that I went to a beach and stood in the shallow water, who cares? When I mention that I surfed, people are mesmerized. Why is this the case? Because, of the general population, a majority have never done it! That's the point I am stressing; who wants the same story as everyone else? Almost all would say "absolutely not, that would be boring". Then why do we constantly shape ourselves in the image of those surrounding us? It is time to leave the safety of the shallow and jump into questionable depths. If you want transformation, meaning and bliss, stop doing the same things that have never led to anything of value. Life is too short to be boring! Tim Robbins' character Andy Dufressne, in the film *The Shawshank Redemption* says it best: "I guess it comes down to a simple choice, really. Get busy living or get busy dying". To live, to grow, to love, to run!

About the Author

Dan Billish is a high school English teacher, cross-country, and track & field coach. He has taught and coached in some capacity for the past 16 years and has found it to be his life work. An avid runner since an early age, he continues to trudge out miles despite his ailing frame. Dan ran at Brother Rice High School in Chicago, Illinois, where he is a current member of the Circle of Champions Athletic Hall of Fame. He spent his collegiate years at Indiana University running under the tutelage of legendary coach Sam Bell and Dr. Robert Chapman. At Indiana, he was a first team All-Big Ten athlete and team captain. As a coach, his teams have had a good deal of success at the state level. Running remains the centerpiece of his life and he uses his experiences to bring strength to others. *To Run* is his first published work.

He lives in the western suburbs of Chicago, Illinois, with his wife Renee, twin sons, Cayden and Lincoln, and his dog, Prints. Follow him on Twitter @Billish12

Made in the USA
Monee, IL
14 December 2019